YOUR UNIQU

OUR UNIQUE DES

QUE DESIGN

FACILITATOR GUIDE

SHIRLEY GILES DAVIS

Your Unique Design Facilitator Guide
© 2020 by Shirley Giles Davis. All Rights Reserved. No portion of this book may be copied, reproduced, or transmitted in any form or by any means without the express written consent of the author.
© Spiritual Gifts Assessment 2017 by Shirley Giles Davis and Allan Harvey. All Rights Reserved. No portion of the gifts assessment may be copied, reproduced, or transmitted in any form or by any means without the express written consent of the authors.

ISBN: 978-0-578-65827-8

All Scriptures referenced are from the New International Version of the Bible, 2011, by Zondervan, unless otherwise noted.
Design by Ashley Anna Matthews.
Design Updated by Bree Van Dyke.

Table of Contents

PREPARING TO OFFER THE YOUR UNIQUE DESIGN CLASS AT YOUR CHURCH

Deciding to offer the Your Unique Design discovery class at your church is just a piece of a bigger process of engaging everyone in meaningful service. The next few pages provide important foundational guidance as you pre-plan.

Some key questions to ask

☐ Does your ministry culture help everyone to understand and live out their unique giftedness for ministry?

☐ Does your church have a system to assist and encourage people in finding meaningful places of service?

☐ How is your desire to offer the Your Unique Design classes and help people discover their gifts connected with the larger vision of seeing your whole church family grow into the image of Jesus Christ?

☐ Is your ultimate goal that these efforts will help people glorify God and serve others in His name-- as an act of worship and as a means of spiritual growth?

☐ Does your church staff welcome and embrace the concept that ALL are called to serve? ALL are gifted?

☐ How well do your staff and ministry leaders embrace their role as equippers of the congregation to do ministry?

☐ Is "ministry" defined at your church by what is done inside AND outside the church walls?

How to implement this discovery process at your church

1. **CREATE A PRAYER TEAM** that will begin praying for the discovery process and planning efforts. Invite people to pray who are passionate about equipping and seeing everyone engaged in meaningful relationships and service in your church and the surrounding community.

2. **INVITE KEY PEOPLE** to be on your Equipping Ministry or Discovery Team. These are people who also see the importance of having this intentional process, ones who are willing to do the collaborating, creating and implementing, and those who have influence in vital areas in your church community.

3. **GAIN SUPPORT** from primary leadership—pastors, department heads, other staff, session, board(s), key influencers.

4. **AS YOU THINK THIS THROUGH**, ask yourselves is our focus simply "plugging people in?" or do we want to be more about "growing disciples more effectively?" Is there a culture in the organization that is about filling slots, or a culture that focuses on helping people understand and live into the high calling described in 1 Peter 2:9: YOU are a "royal priesthood?"

5. **Consider a two-pronged approach:** one that focuses on equipping the congregation for meaningful involvement; the second that focuses on pastors, staff, and ministry leaders to encourage them to adopt the same equipping mindset and make room for others in ministry (Ephesians 4:11-13).

6. **Be clear on your vision and mission:** Also take time, with your team, to articulate key concepts, set specific equipping ministry goals, and develop a realistic (but challenging) action plan.

7. **Create job descriptions** (see sample in Appendix E, pg 86 in this book) for all ministry opportunities at your church (and in the community). Many of these likely exist. Gather them together. See what's missing and fill in the gaps. Get ministry leaders to help with this. Help them understand the importance of inviting specific people to detailed job descriptions. The entire process improves from start to finish once these are in place.

8. **Offer the Your Unique Design two-session course** at a time that it will attract at least 10 people to your first class.

9. **Encourage participation** in the class and the calling/gifts discovery process—so people can discover and/or further clarify their God-given giftedness for ministry and to learn the language of the Body of Christ. As you do, gather gifts, interest, ability, experience information from each person and develop a database. In addition, provide coaching to individuals seeking to connect. (Eventually, you will likely want to have a discovery teaching and organizing team and a coaching team—but, early on, people on your vision team may need to fill these positions until you find additional members.)

10. **From your gathered job descriptions, connect people** in Your Unique Design classes to the positions that are the best fit for them in terms of their calling and gifts. Note: Their place of best fit may sometimes be outside the walls of your church.

11. **Ensure that every invitation to ministry is grounded** in a job description, an intentional, personal invitation, and promised follow-up.

12. **Interview everyone** who is invited and interested. Listen. Be sure that they know the expectations and support provided. Listen for a match between their interests, gifts, and life experience. Prayerfully decide. Remember, desperation never served anyone. Better to leave a position unfilled for a time than push someone into something that's not a fit.

13. **Do your necessary screening** and risk management. Background checks, references, etc. should be mandatory in some serving contexts. Remember to protect your most vulnerable populations and your volunteers.

14. **Once someone is invited** to serve and accepts, orientation and training are essential. Have an orientation and training plan in place or see that each ministry has such a plan.

15. **DETERMINE** what sort of ongoing communication, continuing education, evaluation, and recognition are needed. Make a plan for those. (One of the principal reasons people leave their volunteer positions is that they feel unappreciated and unrecognized.)

16. **OFFER THE *GOD. GIFTS. YOU. YOUR UNIQUE CALLING AND DESIGN*** six-week study (with workbook and accompanying video teaching sessions) so people can go deeper into their understanding of gifts, calling, and purpose.

The goal is to do all of the above well so that you retain these people as equal and growing-in-Christ ministry partners for the long-term.

Inviting People into the Adventure and Growth of Serving

As a ministry leader, you have the privilege of inviting people into the adventure of living as Christ-followers in every corner of their lives. Helping people see their whole lives as ministry, not just what is done in the context of Sunday or church, is a great gift you can give as you disciple them and engage them in your ministry area in various ways.

Your invitation involves many things, including...

INVITING PEOPLE TO UNDERSTAND THAT ALL THEY DO CAN BE VALUED AS WORKING FOR GOD:

COLOSSIANS 3:23-24 Whatever you do, work at it with all your heart, as working for the Lord, not for human masters, since you know that you will receive an inheritance from the Lord as a reward. It is the Lord Christ you are serving.

INVITING PEOPLE TO FIND JOY IN SERVANTHOOD:

ISAIAH 65:14 My servants will sing out of the joy of their hearts...
LUKE 10:1, 17 After this the Lord appointed seventy-two others and sent them two by two ahead of him to every town and place where he was about to go...The seventy-two returned with joy...
JOHN 15:10-12 If you keep my commands, you will remain in my love, just as I have kept my Father's commands and remain in his love. I have told you this so that my joy may be in you and that your joy may be complete. My command is this: Love each other as I have loved you.

INVITING PEOPLE TO UNDERSTAND THAT THEIR SERVICE IS A FORM OF WORSHIP:

ROMANS 12:1 Therefore, I urge you, brothers and sisters, in view of God's mercy, to offer your bodies as a living sacrifice, holy and pleasing to God—this is your true and proper worship.

INVITING PEOPLE TO SEE THAT THEY ARE GRACE-GIVERS:

1 PETER 4:10 Each of you should use whatever gift you have received to serve others, as faithful stewards of God's grace in its various forms.

INVITING PEOPLE INTO GOD'S CALL TO SERVE:

EPHESIANS 4:11-13 So Christ himself gave the apostles, the prophets, the evangelists, the pastors and teachers, to equip his people for works of service, so that the body of Christ may be built up until we all reach unity in the faith and in the knowledge of the Son of God and become mature, attaining to the whole measure of the fullness of Christ.

INVITING PEOPLE INTO THE ADVENTURE OF DISCOVERING AND USING HOW GOD HAS GIFTED THEM:

1 CORINTHIANS 12:7-11 Now to each one the manifestation of the Spirit is given for the common good. To one there is given through the Spirit a message of wisdom, to another a message of knowledge by means of the same Spirit, to another faith by the same Spirit, to another gifts of healing by that one Spirit, to another miraculous powers, to another prophecy, to another distinguishing between spirits, to another speaking in different kinds of tongues, and to still another the interpretation of tongues. All these are the work of one and the same Spirit, and he distributes them to each one, just as he determines.

INVITING PEOPLE TO BE AN INTEGRAL PART OF THE DIVERSE COMMUNITY THAT IS THE BODY OF CHRIST:

1 CORINTHIANS 12:4-6, 12, 14, 18-20, 27 There are different kinds of gifts, but the same Spirit distributes them. There are different kinds of service, but the same Lord. There are different kinds of working, but in all of them and in everyone it is the same God at work. Just as a body, though one, has many parts, but all its many parts form one body, so it is with Christ…Even so the body is not made up of one part but of many. But in fact God has placed the parts in the body, every one of them, just as he wanted them to be. If they were all one part, where would the body be? As it is, there are many parts, but one body…Now you are the body of Christ, and each one of you is a part of it.

MOST PEOPLE VOLUNTEER BECAUSE THEY WERE ASKED!*

So, how many people have you ASKED to be involved in ministry this week? This month? If your job is to equip others for ministry (Ephesians 4:11-13), how are you being intentional about equipping?

There is simply no substitute for a personal appeal. But not just an appeal based on your ministry needs. It is a thoughtful request rooted in a number of key things (that also make the "yes" more likely):

PRAY: Pray that God would direct you to the right people and the right people to you. You truly do not want the wrong person in the wrong place for all the wrong reasons. Prayer also helps you let go of the outcome, so that when you are inviting people, you can leave their decision in God's hands.

FIND AND CONNECT WITH THEIR INTERESTS AND DESIRES: Yes, people may care about your ministry but, if they are passionate about it or about some aspect of it, they will more likely want to be involved and will give more of themselves, go deeper, and stay longer.

BE CLEAR: People commit to a specific "ask." Be clear on your expectations in terms of skills, experience, time commitment. Have a clear job description for them.

GIVE THEM TIME: Ask them to prayerfully consider involvement and give them a week or so to reflect on the job description and your request. You are much less likely to get the knee-jerk "no" if you give people the space to pray and the freedom to say "no."

THINK OF EACH "ASK" AS AN EDUCATIONAL OR DISCIPLESHIP MOMENT: Even if you have to ask 12 people to get two "yeses," you have let 12 people know of your need, you have asked them to pray about that need and your ministry, you have asked them to spend time reflecting with God on His call and gifting and their availability (a teachable moment, often), you have acknowledged their unique value simply by reaching out and asking, and, if you promise to pray for them, you have offered them a pastoral care moment. So, even if it ends up as a "no," you have done meaningful, relational, caring things to further include these people in your community.

THINK CREATIVELY: If you get many "no's," do you need to revisit that job description and split it into two so that people with less time might be able to do part of it? Can it be done by a couple, a small group, or a family? Are you being clear and specific enough in your "ask," or might it be too ambiguous for people to feel willing to commit to?

Better yet, have one of your faithful, satisfied, passionate volunteers do the asking for you. A satisfied volunteer is the best recruiter.

71% of those who were asked said "yes" to volunteering, vs. 29%. From the document Giving and Volunteering in the United States

GETTING PEOPLE CONNECTED

FIND A PLACE FOR NEW PEOPLE in ministry, especially new members and visitors—those who are "eagerly leaning forward." Create ways to gather their names and interest information and then contact them and connect them A.S.A.P.

CREATE A SPIRITUAL GIFTS DISCOVERY PROCESS at your church, using Your Unique Design materials and resources from GodGiftsYou.com.

CREATE A HOTLIST of Ministry Opportunities and ask each ministry area to provide "job listings." Encourage all ministries to always be thinking of where their ministry gaps are and what kind of person could help fill those gaps. Make sure these needs are on the Hotlist…and, when someone responds with interest, follow up with them in a timely fashion.

IF YOUR CHURCH OFFERS PLACES OF CONNECTION/fellowship/learning (small groups, classes, mentoring, etc.) with an "open chair" policy, consider creating a Hotlist of Fellowship/Learning Opportunities to make it easier for people to find those places of connection.

CREATE AND MAKE USE OF A DATABASE. Ask people to provide information about their ministry interests, talents, gifts, etc. and create a church-wide database that can be used to find the right person for the job!

COMMUNICATE NEEDS AND AREAS for people to serve. Use all methods of communication, knowing that repetition helps. Never sound desperate, and always let people know the benefits of getting involved. Use social media, your church's website, your church's phone app, bulletins, pulpit announcements, emails, texts, fliers, and face-to-face and phone communication.

CONNECT IN MEANINGFUL WAYS with the community. Add information about local nonprofit agencies with current needs to your Hotlist of Ministry Opportunities. Create ongoing relationships with these agencies.

PROVIDE ONE OR MORE ALL-CHURCH DAYS OF SERVICE—a great way to build community amongst your congregation and friends as well as to serve in tangible ways where there are needs. Start first with those outside agencies and organizations with whom you have a relationship.

INVITE PEOPLE TO GET INVOLVED based on giftedness and passion for ministry. Make sure that what you ask them to do is not only a "fit" but is also meaningful and appreciated by you.

OFFERING THE YOUR UNIQUE DESIGN CLASS

The Your Unique Design course runs 1 to 1.5 hours per session. Discuss with your team what might be the best timing for people at your church to best participate. Consider time of year—is it better in the Fall when people are thinking about getting involved? In the Spring? On consecutive Sunday mornings or Sunday evenings? Is there a time when your congregation is used to partaking in new classes?

Promote the class through all avenues

- On your church website.
- Via your all-church communication outlets—email blasts, social media posts, newsletters, etc.
- Announce in worship and other church gatherings.
- Put in your bulletin prior to and including the weeks you wish people to register.
- Identify people you know might benefit from the class and personally invite them. Have your team do the same.

Sample class worship/bulletin/email announcement language

We are excited to offer the new two-part Your Unique Design class—on [DATE] at [TIME] at [LOCATION]. All materials will be provided. Our hope for these two weeks is to help you further explore God's call on your life, how you're gifted by Him, and how to connect that to doing life and ministry at work, in the church, and in the community in ways that honor Him and others.

Register here: [provide information about how they can register—in person? Online? Via email/phone?]

Possible additions to the announcement

You will have the opportunity to complete a spiritual gifts assessment, debrief your gifts, and discuss what you learn within the context of a small group.

Additionally, we'll discuss important foundational concepts of God's unique design of each person, what it means to be "called," equipped, to serve, and live as the Body of Christ.

What part of the Body are you? Come and find out. We'd love to have you there!

Prior to your first class

Review the first page of each script for the supplies you will need for each class. Allow enough time for your book orders to arrive prior to the first class.

Determine in advance if you will
- Provide the books and class to participants at no cost to them.
- Ask participants to pay for the books.
- Ask participants to pay a class fee to cover books and incidentals.
- Ask participants to consider giving a donation to offset costs.

Send out reminders—email, social media, other—to class registrants—reminding them of the day, time, location, and any other pertinent information.

Determine if you want to have participants take the GodGiftsYou.com spiritual gifts assessment in advance and send that link to those who register. Remind them to bring their results with them. Otherwise, ask each participant to bring an internet-capable device with them (phone, tablet, laptop, etc.).

On the following pages are the scripts for each class.

YOUR UNIQUE DESIGN CLASS FACILITATOR SCRIPTS
SESSION 1:   INTRODUCING GIFTS

Preparation/Set-up

Need:

>   Projector or TV/Monitor.
>   Screen.
>   HDMI connector and cable.
>   Laptop with class slides (download from GodGiftsYou.com Resources page).
>   Backup USB w/slides.
>   Microphone/sound system.
>   Remote control for laptop with back-up batteries and USB connector.
>   Pens.
>   Your Unique Design Class Guide books—one per participant.
>   Enough 8 colored-pencil packages for one box per table.
>   One coloring book page per person. This is Appendix A in your Facilitator Guide.
>   Refreshments for the class (if desired) and cups/plates/napkins/utensils.
>   Table of Resources, if providing. (Might include lists of serving opportunities, recommended books, next steps, etc.)

Classroom set-up: Music stand or podium for scripts, projection screen, cart for laptop and projector or laptop connected to a TV, Your Unique Design workbooks—one for each participant, round tables (or rectangular) with seats for 4-6 at each table, a table for any additional resources and name tags, a table for cups/plates/water/goodies (if you have a plan to ask people to provide such), coffee/tea cart.

Prior to class:

>   Put pens on tables.
>   Put one box of colored pencils per table.
>   Put coloring pages on tables - one per person if doing warm-up exercise.
>   Note: take time to manually add page numbers throughout script, based on the latest version of the workbook provided to participants.

Warm Up Exercise

- At your tables, each person choose the colored pencil that represents his/her favorite color.
- Together with those at your table, using only the favorite colors chosen by the 4-6 of you, color in the appropriate sections of the coloring page provided.
- Are you able to complete the whole picture with your selected colors?
- Now, have each table hold up their colored pages.
- Within the room, would you be able to complete the picture with all the colors represented?

CLASS GUIDE

Session One
Introducing Gifts

Group Exercise

WRITE DOWN ONE THING YOU HOPE TO GET OUT OF THESE TWO SESSIONS ABOUT YOUR OWN UNIQUE DESIGN:

Biblical Foundations

YOU ARE UNIQUE: CREATED UNIQUELY AND SPECIALLY BY GOD

PSALM 139:13-18 | For you created my inmost being; you knit me together in my mother's womb. I praise you because I am fearfully and wonderfully made; your works are wonderful, I know that full well. My frame was not hidden from you when I was made in the secret place. When I was woven together in the depths of the earth, your eyes saw my unformed body. All the days ordained for me were written in your book before one of them came to be.

YOU ARE LOVED

EPHESIANS 3:17-19 | Paul prays that we "may have power... to grasp how wide and long and high and deep is the love of Christ, and to know this love that surpasses knowledge..."

EPHESIANS 5:1 | Calls us "dearly loved children."

SESSION 1

INTRO

LET ME TELL YOU A LITTLE BIT ABOUT MYSELF
[Instructor give a BRIEF personal intro. as it relates to this class.]

BUT REALLY THIS CLASS IS ABOUT GIFTS. GOD. AND *YOU*.

LET'S DO A QUICK WARM-UP EXERCISE. [Leaders—feel free to change/adapt this exercise if you wish. The point is to show the diversity in the room and the importance of each and every person.]

- At your tables, each person choose the colored pencil that represents his/her favorite color.
- Using only your favorite color, color in the appropriate sections of the coloring page provided.
- Are you able to complete the whole picture with your selected color?
- Would your table be able to complete the whole picture with just your table's colors?
- Now, have each table hold up their colored pages.
- Within the room, would you be able to complete the picture with all the colors represented?

THIS IS A VISUAL DEMONSTRATION OF THE CONCEPT THAT YOU AND I ARE EACH ESSENTIAL MEMBERS OF THE BODY OF CHRIST—A UNIQUE AND VIBRANT COLOR THAT CONTRIBUTES SOMETHING TO THE BIGGER PICTURE, IF YOU WILL.

OUR HOPE FOR THESE TWO WEEKS IS TO HELP YOU FURTHER EXPLORE GOD'S CALL ON YOUR LIFE, HOW YOU'RE GIFTED BY HIM, AND HOW TO CONNECT ALL THAT TO DOING LIFE AND MINISTRY IN THE CHURCH AND THE COMMUNITY IN WAYS THAT HONOR HIM AND OTHERS. AND, WE HOPE THAT YOU WILL HELP ONE ANOTHER WITH THOSE DISCOVERIES.

TAKE A MOMENT TO WRITE DOWN ONE THING YOU HOPE TO GET OUT OF THIS CLASS IN YOUR BOOK ON PAGE 9.

IN YOUR GROUPS, INTRODUCE YOURSELVES AND SHARE THAT ONE THING WITH EACH OTHER. [If the class is small—less than 10 people, go around the room and have each person state their name. If not small, have them say their names to others at their tables.]

Unique

- **Psalm 139:13-18** For you created my inmost being; you knit me together in my mother's womb. I praise you because I am fearfully and wonderfully made; your works are wonderful, I know that full well. My frame was not hidden from you when I was made in the secret place. When I was woven together in the depths of the earth, your eyes saw my unformed body. All the days ordained for me were written in your book before one of them came to be.

Loved

- **Ephesians 3:17-19** Paul prays that we "may have power...to grasp how wide and long and high and deep is the love of Christ, and to know this love that surpasses knowledge..."
- **Ephesians 5:1** calls us God's "dearly loved children."

HAND
ARM

Called...Chosen...Set Apart

- **1 Corinthians 6:11** now your sins have been washed away... you have been set apart for God.
- **Ephesians 2:10** For we are God's handiwork, created in Christ Jesus to do good works, which God prepared in advance for us to do.

Session One
Introducing Gifts

Group Exercise

WRITE DOWN ONE THING YOU HOPE TO GET OUT OF THESE TWO SESSIONS ABOUT YOUR OWN UNIQUE DESIGN:

Biblical Foundations

YOU ARE UNIQUE: CREATED UNIQUELY AND SPECIALLY BY GOD

PSALM 139:13-18 | For you created my inmost being; you knit me together in my mother's womb. I praise you because I am fearfully and wonderfully made; your works are wonderful, I know that full well. My frame was not hidden from you when I was made in the secret place. When I was woven together in the depths of the earth, your eyes saw my unformed body. All the days ordained for me were written in your book before one of them came to be

YOU ARE LOVED

EPHESIANS 3:17-19 | Paul prays that we "may have power... to grasp how wide and long and high and deep is the love of Christ, and to know this love that surpasses knowledge ..."

EPHESIANS 5:1 | Calls us "dearly loved children."

YOU ARE CALLED...CHOSEN...SET APART

1 CORINTHIANS 6:11 | Now your sins have been washed away...you have been set apart for God.

EPHESIANS 2:10 | For we are God's handiwork, created in Christ Jesus to do good works, which God prepared in advance for us to do.

HE CALLS...AND...HE EQUIPS

HEBREWS 13:20-21 | Now may the God of peace, who through the blood of the eternal covenant brought back from the dead our Lord Jesus, that great Shepherd of the sheep, equip you with everything good for doing his will, and may he work in us what is pleasing to him, through Jesus Christ, to whom be glory for ever and ever. Amen.

SPIRITUAL GIFTS

Greek Terminology:

The primary scriptural basis for spiritual gifts is found in:

Romans 12
1 Corinthians 12-14
Ephesians 4
1 Peter 4

Spiritual Gifts are (from those passages):
- Special abilities; spiritual, beyond our natural talents.
- Given distributed by God according to His choosing, His grace, His mercy.
- Through the Holy Spirit — Spirit empowered.
- To each and every believer in Jesus.
- In order to be used to glorify God.
- For the common good and strengthening of the Body of Christ.
- Given to you for others; you benefit but it's not about you.

BEFORE WE GET INTO THE SPECIFICS OF GIFTS, IT'S IMPORTANT TO TALK ABOUT SOME FOUNDATIONAL THINGS: (BY THE WAY, THERE ARE A NUMBER OF VERSES THAT SUPPORT EACH OF THESE CONCEPTS. HOWEVER, IN THE INTEREST OF TIME, WE WILL FOCUS ON ONLY ONE OR TWO FOR EACH POINT.)

YOU ARE UNIQUE.
YOU ARE CREATED UNIQUELY AND SPECIALLY BY GOD: [ask someone to read aloud.]

- PSALM 139:13-16 FOR YOU CREATED MY INMOST BEING; YOU KNIT ME TOGETHER IN MY MOTHER'S WOMB. I PRAISE YOU BECAUSE I AM FEARFULLY AND WONDERFULLY MADE; YOUR WORKS ARE WONDERFUL, I KNOW THAT FULL WELL. MY FRAME WAS NOT HIDDEN FROM YOU WHEN I WAS MADE IN THE SECRET PLACE. WHEN I WAS WOVEN TOGETHER IN THE DEPTHS OF THE EARTH, YOUR EYES SAW MY UNFORMED BODY. ALL THE DAYS ORDAINED FOR ME WERE WRITTEN IN YOUR BOOK BEFORE ONE OF THEM CAME TO BE.

    - YOU ARE KNOWN INSIDE AND OUT.
    - YOU'RE NOT AN ACCIDENT.
    - GOD HAS BEEN PURPOSEFUL IN CREATING YOU WITH THE PARTICULAR WAYS YOU INTERACT WITH THE WORLD AROUND YOU.

YOU ARE LOVED.

- EPHESIANS 3:17-19 PAUL PRAYS THAT WE "MAY HAVE POWER... TO GRASP HOW WIDE AND LONG AND HIGH AND DEEP IS THE LOVE OF CHRIST, AND TO KNOW THIS LOVE THAT SURPASSES KNOWLEDGE..."

- EPHESIANS 5:1 CALLS US "DEARLY LOVED CHILDREN."

YOU ARE CALLED...CHOSEN...SET APART.

- 1 CORINTHIANS 6:11 NOW YOUR SINS HAVE BEEN WASHED AWAY...YOU HAVE BEEN SET APART FOR GOD.

- EPHESIANS 2:10 FOR WE ARE GOD'S HANDIWORK, CREATED IN CHRIST JESUS TO DO GOOD WORKS, WHICH GOD PREPARED IN ADVANCE FOR US TO DO.

Your Unique Design: Guide

1 Corinthians 6:11 now your sins have been washed away...you have been set apart for God.

Ephesians 2:10 For we are God's handiwork, created in Christ Jesus to do good works, which God prepared in advance for us to do.

Called...Chosen...Set Apart

Hebrews 13:20-21 Now may the God of peace, who through the blood of the eternal covenant brought back from the dead our Lord Jesus, that great Shepherd of the sheep, equip you with everything good for doing his will, and may he work in us what is pleasing to him, through Jesus Christ, to whom be glory for ever and ever. Amen.

Equips

Charis → Charismata

Pneuma → Pneumatikon

Romans 12   1 Corinthians 12-14
Ephesians 4   1 Peter 4

YOUR UNIQUE DESIGN

YOU ARE CALLED...CHOSEN...SET APART

1 CORINTHIANS 6:11 | Now your sins have been washed away...you have been set apart for God.

EPHESIANS 2:10 | For we are God's handiwork, created in Christ Jesus to do good works, which God prepared in advance for us to do.

HE CALLS...AND...HE EQUIPS

HEBREWS 13:20-21| Now may the God of peace, who through the blood of the eternal covenant brought back from the dead our Lord Jesus, that great Shepherd of the sheep, equip you with everything good for doing his will, and may he work in us what is pleasing to him, through Jesus Christ, to whom be glory for ever and ever. Amen.

SPIRITUAL GIFTS

Greek Terminology:

The primary scriptural basis for spiritual gifts is found in:

Romans 12
1 Corinthians 12-14
Ephesians 4
1 Peter 4

Spiritual Gifts are (from those passages):
- Special abilities; spiritual, beyond our natural talents.
- Given/distributed by God according to His choosing, His grace, His mercy.
- Through the Holy Spirit — Spirit empowered.
- To each and every believer in Jesus.
- In order to be used to glorify God.
- For the common good and strengthening of the Body of Christ.
- Given to you for others; you benefit but it's not about you.

SO YOU AND I ARE SET APART, CHOSEN BY GOD...NOT BASED ON OUR ABILITIES OR SUCCESSES OR FAILURES.

CALLING REALLY IS ABOUT GOD SAYING "I HAVE A PLAN AND IT INVOLVES YOU"...BUT THEN HE DOESN'T SAY "AND NOW YOU'RE ON YOUR OWN TO ACCOMPLISH THAT PLAN." HE SAYS "MY PLAN INVOLVES YOU AND I WILL EQUIP YOU TO BE ABLE TO DO WHAT I ASK YOU TO DO."

HE CALLS...AND...HE EQUIPS. [Ask a class participant to read the following verse aloud.]

- **HEBREWS 13:20-21** NOW MAY THE GOD OF PEACE, WHO THROUGH THE BLOOD OF THE ETERNAL COVENANT BROUGHT BACK FROM THE DEAD OUR LORD JESUS, THAT GREAT SHEPHERD OF THE SHEEP, EQUIP YOU WITH EVERYTHING GOOD FOR DOING HIS WILL, AND MAY HE WORK IN US WHAT IS PLEASING TO HIM, THROUGH JESUS CHRIST, TO WHOM BE GLORY FOR EVER AND EVER. AMEN.

AND A PIECE OF THAT EQUIPMENT IS SPIRITUAL GIFTS.

THE WORD FOR GRACE IN GREEK IS CHARIS. [PRONOUNCED KAR-EE-S]. IN THE NEW TESTAMENT, ONE OF THE WORDS USED FOR SPIRITUAL GIFTS IS CHARISMATA. SO GIFTS ARE ROOTED IN GOD'S GRACE AND GENEROSITY TO US AND ARE A WAY WE EXHIBIT GOD'S GRACE AND GENEROSITY TO OTHERS.

THE WORD FOR HOLY SPIRIT IN GREEK IS PNEUMA. THE OTHER WORD USED FOR SPIRITUAL GIFTS IS PNEUMATIKON, MEANING THEY ARE NOT ONLY GRACE-GIFTS BUT ARE ALSO GIVEN AND EMPOWERED AND DIRECTED BY THE HOLY SPIRIT—NOT BY US.

THE SCRIPTURAL BASIS FOR SPIRITUAL GIFTS IS FOUND IN:
- ROMANS 12
- 1 CORINTHIANS 12-14
- EPHESIANS 4
- 1 PETER 4

Spiritual Gifts are

☐ Special abilities
☐ Distributed by God according to His choosing, His grace, His mercy
☐ through His Holy Spirit
☐ to each and every believer in Jesus
☐ in order to be used to glorify God
☐ and for the common good and strengthening of the Body of Christ

---

1 Corinthians 12

v. 1 Now about the gifts of the Spirit, brothers and sisters, I do not want you to be uninformed.

v. 4-11 There are different kinds of gifts, but the same Spirit distributes them. There are different kinds of service, but the same Lord. There are different kinds of working, but in all of them and in everyone it is the same God at work. Now to each one the manifestation of the Spirit is given for the common good. To one there is given through the Spirit a message of wisdom, to another a message of knowledge by means of the same Spirit, to another faith by the same Spirit, to another gifts of healing by that one Spirit, to another miraculous powers, to another prophecy, to another distinguishing between spirits, to another speaking in different kinds of tongues [languages] and to still another the interpretation of tongues [languages]. All these are the work of one and the same Spirit, and he distributes them to each one, just as he determines.

YOUR UNIQUE DESIGN

YOU ARE CALLED....CHOSEN....SET APART

1 CORINTHIANS 6:11 | Now your sins have been washed away...you have been set apart for God.

EPHESIANS 2:10 | For we are God's handiwork, created in Christ Jesus to do good works, which God prepared in advance for us to do.

HE CALLS....AND....HE EQUIPS

HEBREWS 13:20-21 | Now may the God of peace, who through the blood of the eternal covenant brought back from the dead our Lord Jesus, that great Shepherd of the sheep, equip you with everything good for doing his will, and may he work in us what is pleasing to him, through Jesus Christ, to whom be glory for ever and ever. Amen.

SPIRITUAL GIFTS

Greek Terminology:

The primary scriptural basis for spiritual gifts is found in:

Romans 12
1 Corinthians 12-14
Ephesians 4
1 Peter 4

Spiritual Gifts are (from those passages):
- Special abilities; spiritual, beyond our natural talents.
- Given/distributed by God according to His choosing, His grace, His mercy.
- Through the Holy Spirit — Spirit empowered.
- To each and every believer in Jesus.
- In order to be used to glorify God.
- For the common good and strengthening of the Body of Christ.
- Given to you for others; you benefit but it's not about you.

CLASS GUIDE

1 CORINTHIANS 12:1 | Now about the gifts of the Spirit, brothers and sisters, I do not want you to be uninformed...

1 CORINTHIANS 12:4-11 | There are different kinds of gifts, but the same Spirit distributes them. There are different kinds of service, but the same Lord. There are different kinds of working, but in all of them and in everyone it is the same God at work. Now to each one the manifestation of the Spirit is given for the common good. To one there is given through the Spirit a message of wisdom, to another a message of knowledge by means of the same Spirit, to another faith by the same Spirit, to another gifts of healing by that one Spirit, to another miraculous powers, to another prophecy, to another distinguishing between spirits, to another speaking in different kinds of tongues [languages] and to still another the interpretation of tongues [languages]. All these are the work of one and the same Spirit, and he distributes them to each one, just as he determines.

CALLED TO SERVE CHRIST WITH THE WHOLE OF OURSELVES

ROMANS 12:1-2 | Therefore, I urge you, brothers and sisters, in view of God's mercy, to offer your bodies as a living sacrifice, holy and pleasing to God—this is your true and proper worship. Do not conform to the pattern of this world, but be transformed by the renewing of your mind. Then you will be able to test and approve what God's will is—his good, pleasing and perfect will.

COLOSSIANS 3:23-24 | Whatever you do, work at it with all of your heart, as working for the Lord, not for human masters, since you know that you will receive an inheritance from the Lord as a reward. It is the Lord Christ you are serving.

SPIRITUAL GIFTS ARE (PRIMARILY FROM THOSE PASSAGES):
- SPECIAL ABILITIES; SPIRITUAL--BEYOND OUR NATURAL TALENTS.
- GIVEN/DISTRIBUTED BY GOD ACCORDING TO HIS CHOOSING, HIS GRACE, HIS MERCY.
- THROUGH THE HOLY SPIRIT--SPIRIT-EMPOWERED.
- TO EACH AND EVERY BELIEVER IN JESUS.
- IN ORDER TO BE USED TO GLORIFY GOD (1 PETER 4:11).
- AND FOR THE COMMON GOOD AND STRENGTHENING OF THE BODY OF CHRIST. (EPH. 4:11-13).
- GIVEN TO YOU FOR OTHERS; YOU BENEFIT BUT IT'S NOT ABOUT YOU.

PLEASE FOLLOW ALONG WITH ME AS I READ 1 CORINTHIANS 12:1, 4-11 [I'M USING THE NEW INTERNATIONAL VERSION (NIV) 2011.] [Note: 1 Corinthians 12-14 is the most thorough teaching about spiritual gifts in Scripture. *Alternative*: Have them read individually to themselves.]

- **1 CORINTHIANS 12:1** NOW ABOUT THE GIFTS OF THE SPIRIT, BROTHERS AND SISTERS, I DO NOT WANT YOU TO BE UNINFORMED...

...V. 4-11 THERE ARE DIFFERENT KINDS OF GIFTS, BUT THE SAME SPIRIT DISTRIBUTES THEM. THERE ARE DIFFERENT KINDS OF SERVICE, BUT THE SAME LORD. THERE ARE DIFFERENT KINDS OF WORKING, BUT IN ALL OF THEM AND IN EVERYONE IT IS THE SAME GOD AT WORK. NOW TO EACH ONE THE MANIFESTATION OF THE SPIRIT IS GIVEN FOR THE COMMON GOOD. TO ONE THERE IS GIVEN THROUGH THE SPIRIT A MESSAGE OF WISDOM, TO ANOTHER A MESSAGE OF KNOWLEDGE BY MEANS OF THE SAME SPIRIT, TO ANOTHER FAITH BY THE SAME SPIRIT, TO ANOTHER GIFTS OF HEALING BY THAT ONE SPIRIT, TO ANOTHER MIRACULOUS POWERS, TO ANOTHER PROPHECY, TO ANOTHER DISTINGUISHING BETWEEN SPIRITS, TO ANOTHER SPEAKING IN DIFFERENT KINDS OF TONGUES [LANGUAGES] AND TO STILL ANOTHER THE INTERPRETATION OF TONGUES [LANGUAGES]. ALL THESE ARE THE WORK OF ONE AND THE SAME SPIRIT, AND HE DISTRIBUTES THEM TO EACH ONE, JUST AS HE DETERMINES.

ASK: WHAT STANDS OUT TO YOU IN THIS PASSAGE ABOUT GIFTS?

With whole self

- **Romans 12:1-2** Therefore, I urge you, brothers and sisters, in view of God's mercy, to offer your bodies as a living sacrifice, holy and pleasing to God—this is your true and proper worship. Do not conform to the pattern of this world, but be transformed by the renewing of your mind. Then you will be able to test and approve what God's will is—his good, pleasing and perfect will.

- **Colossians 3:23-24** Whatever you do, work heartily, as for the Lord and not for men, knowing that from the Lord you will receive the inheritance as your reward. You are serving the Lord Christ.

---

1 CORINTHIANS 12:1 | Now about the gifts of the Spirit, brothers and sisters, I do not want you to be uninformed...

1 CORINTHIANS 12:4-11 | There are different kinds of gifts, but the same Spirit distributes them. There are different kinds of service, but the same Lord. There are different kinds of working, but in all of them and in everyone it is the same God at work. Now to each one the manifestation of the Spirit is given for the common good. To one there is given through the Spirit a message of wisdom, to another a message of knowledge by means of the same Spirit, to another faith by the same Spirit, to another gifts of healing by that one Spirit, to another miraculous powers, to another prophecy, to another distinguishing between spirits, to another speaking in different kinds of tongues [languages] and to still another the interpretation of tongues [languages]. All these are the work of one and the same Spirit, and he distributes them to each one, just as he determines.

CALLED TO SERVE CHRIST WITH THE WHOLE OF OURSELVES

ROMANS 12:1-2 | Therefore, I urge you, brothers and sisters, in view of God's mercy, to offer your bodies as a living sacrifice, holy and pleasing to God—this is your true and proper worship. Do not conform to the pattern of this world, but be transformed by the renewing of your mind. Then you will be able to test and approve what God's will is—his good, pleasing and perfect will.

COLOSSIANS 3:23-24 | Whatever you do, work at it with all of your heart, as working for the Lord, not for human masters, since you know that you will receive an inheritance from the Lord as a reward. It is the Lord Christ you are serving.

WE ARE CALLED TO FOLLOW/TO SERVE CHRIST WITH THE WHOLE OF OURSELVES.

- **ROMANS 12:1-2** THEREFORE, I URGE YOU, BROTHERS AND SISTERS, IN VIEW OF GOD'S MERCY, TO OFFER YOUR BODIES AS A LIVING SACRIFICE, HOLY AND PLEASING TO GOD—THIS IS YOUR TRUE AND PROPER WORSHIP. DO NOT CONFORM TO THE PATTERN OF THIS WORLD, BUT BE TRANSFORMED BY THE RENEWING OF YOUR MIND. THEN YOU WILL BE ABLE TO TEST AND APPROVE WHAT GOD'S WILL IS—HIS GOOD, PLEASING AND PERFECT WILL.

- **COLOSSIANS 3:23-24** WHATEVER YOU DO, WORK HEARTILY, AS FOR THE LORD AND NOT FOR MEN, KNOWING THAT FROM THE LORD YOU WILL RECEIVE AN INHERITANCE AS YOUR REWARD. YOU ARE SERVING THE LORD CHRIST.

ACCORDING TO THESE PASSAGES SERVICE IS AN EXPECTATION FOR ALL OF US (NOT OPTIONAL)

...AND IT GROWS OUT OF OUR RESPONSE TO A GRACIOUS, GENEROUS GOD...

SERVING IN GOD'S WILL IS TRUE AND ACCEPTABLE WORSHIP, PART OF OFFERING OUR WHOLE SELVES TO GOD.

THIS WORSHIP ENCOMPASSES EVERYTHING WE DO IN OUR LIVES, INSIDE AND OUTSIDE THE WALLS OF THE CHURCH.

GIFTS AND CALL ARE FOR WHAT? TO SERVE!!

[For classes where the assessment was given as homework, skip past this next section to the Spiritual Gifts Overview.]

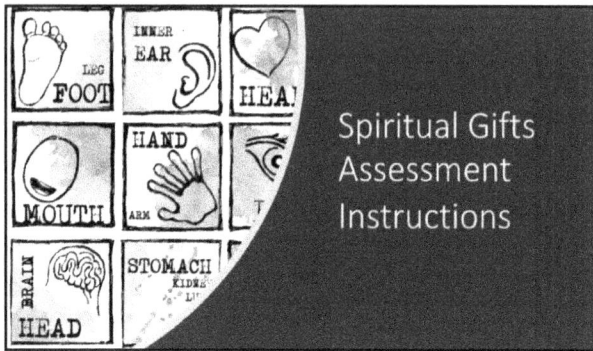

Spiritual Gifts Assessment Instructions

YOUR UNIQUE DESIGN

Spiritual Gifts Assessment

Go to GODGIFTSYOU.COM and click on Assessment. Once you complete all of the questions, you will receive a results page as well as an email containing those same scores. Take a moment to record your highest and lowest scoring gifts below:

Your Spiritual Gifts Assessment Results

SPIRITUAL GIFTS	TOP 3-5 (A-W)	LOW 2 (A-S)	GIFTS AFFIRMED BY OTHERS
A | ADMINISTRATION			
B | APOSTLESHIP			
C | ARTISTIC EXPRESSION			
D | CRAFTSMANSHIP			
E | DISCERNMENT			
F | EVANGELISM			
G | EXHORTATION			
H | FAITH			
I | GIVING			
J | HELPS			
K | HOSPITALITY			
L | INTERCESSION			
M | KNOWLEDGE			
N | LEADERSHIP			
O | MERCY			
P | PROPHECY			
Q | SHEPHERDING			
R | TEACHING			
S | WISDOM			
T | HEALING			
U | MIRACULOUS POWERS			
V | TONGUES			
W | INTERPRETATION OF TONGUES			

(Alternative: Take the same gifts assessment and score it yourself. See Appendix A on page 33.)

INSTRUCTIONS FOR SPIRITUAL GIFT ASSESSMENT (15 MINUTES)

RESPOND TO EACH QUESTION IN THE ASSESSMENT NOT HOW YOU'D LIKE TO BE...BUT HOW YOU ARE. [Explain Scale 0-5. Tell them to USE the Zeros!]

TWO OPTIONS:

1. THEY CAN USE THE FREE ONLINE ASSESSMENT—ON THEIR SMARTPHONES, TABLETS, OR LAPTOPS.

Direct them to GodGiftsYou.com and have them click on Assessment. [This option is fastest and easiest.] Once they have completed all of the questions, they will get a results page as well as an email containing those same results.

Have them take a moment to record that information on the chart on page 12 in their participants' guide.

[Explain A-S and A-W instructions relative to high and low scoring.]

2. THEY ARE ALSO WELCOME TO COMPLETE THE PAPER ASSESSMENT IN THEIR WORKBOOKS—PAGES 33-34, APPENDIX A, IN THEIR CLASS GUIDE. [This is Appendix B in your Facilitator's Guide.]

[Note: some people may need more time than 15 minutes if they do the one in the book since they have to do their own scoring. The online version does the scoring for them.]

[After 10 minutes have elapsed, remind class they have 5 minutes remaining.]

[For those who appear to finish quickly, suggest they take some time to look up the definitions and descriptions of their top-scoring gifts on the Spiritual Gifts Overview handout.]

[Call time at 15 minutes]

Spiritual Gifts Overview

Jot in
- Your gifts as we come to them
- The names of people who you believe have that gift

Spiritual Gifts Overview

Gift	Brief Definition Those with gifts of...	Description	Someone with Gift:
Administration	...bring efficiency and order to the church and to other organizations. These are usually the planners, goal-setters, or managers. They look for new ways to help people and tasks be more effective.	Organizer Strategizer Developer	
Apostleship	...introduce new ministries to the church. They blaze new trails, pioneer new endeavors, and step out into uncharted territory. They may have a great desire to reach out to unreached peoples and to spread the vision of the mission of the church.	Starter Entrepre-neur Pioneer	
Artistic Expression	...have a special ability to communicate God's message through the fine arts, including drama, creative writing, music, and drawing. Through their God-given creativity, they use their gifts to draw others in and focus on God, His creation, and His message.	Expressive Innovative Creative	
Craftsmanship	...are uniquely skilled at working with raw materials, helping to create things that are used for ministry or that help meet tangible needs. They can be found fixing, remodeling, and sprucing up buildings, and/or creating and stitching items--honoring God and ben-efiting His people in practical ways.	Skilled Creative Resourceful	
Discernment	...distinguish between good and evil, truth and error, right and wrong. These people provide much-needed insight, point out inconsistencies in the teaching of God's Word, challenge deceitfulness in others, help sort out impure motives from pure ones, and identify spiritual warfare.	Intuitive Perceptive Sensitive	

SPIRITUAL GIFTS OVERVIEW (LARGE GROUP EXERCISE)

NOW, TURN TO P. 13 THE SPIRITUAL GIFTS OVERVIEW IN YOUR WORKBOOK. WE'RE GOING TO FLY THROUGH THIS CHART PRIMARILY TO HELP YOU GET FAMILIAR WITH A DEFINITION OF EACH OF THE GIFTS.

[Note: this is Appendix C in your Facilitator's Guide.]

AS WE DO,

- JOT IN YOUR GIFTS AS WE COME TO THEM.
- IN ADDITION, ONE OF THE IMPORTANT PIECES OF LIVING AS THE BODY OF CHRIST IS RECOGNIZING AND AFFIRMING GIFTS IN OTHERS.
- AS I BRIEFLY DEFINE EACH GIFT, IT MAY BRING TO MIND A PERSON WITH THAT GIFT.
- JOT IN THE NAMES OF THOSE PEOPLE.

[Instructors: provide an example for one or two of these—not all—as you go along]

THOSE WITH THE GIFT OF...

ADMINISTRATION

BRING EFFICIENCY AND ORDER. THESE ARE USUALLY THE PLANNERS, ORGANIZERS, OR MANAGERS. THEY HELP THE CHURCH AND OTHER ORGANIZATIONS BE MORE EFFECTIVE.

APOSTLESHIP

INTRODUCE NEW MINISTRIES TO THE CHURCH. THEY ARE PIONEERS, OPENING UP NEW AREAS OF MINISTRY OFTEN IN THE CONTEXT OF GOD'S MISSION.

ARTISTIC EXPRESSION

HAVE A SPECIAL ABILITY TO COMMUNICATE GOD'S MESSAGE AND BRING OTHERS CLOSER TO GOD THROUGH THE FINE ARTS, INCLUDING DRAMA, CREATIVE WRITING, MUSIC, AND DRAWING.

CRAFTSMANSHIP

ARE UNIQUELY SKILLED AT CRAFTING THINGS FOR MINISTRY OR THAT HELP MEET TANGIBLE NEEDS. EXAMPLES WOULD INCLUDE FIXING UP BUILDINGS, AND/OR CREATING AND STITCHING ITEMS.

Gift	Brief Definition Those with gifts of..	Description	Someone with Gift:
Administration	..bring efficiency and order to the church and to other organizations. These are usually the planners, goal-setters, or managers. They look for new ways to help people and tasks be more effective.	Organizer Strategizer Developer	
Apostleship	..introduce new ministries to the church. They blaze new trails, pioneer new endeavors, and step out into uncharted territory. They may have a great desire to reach out to unreached peoples and to spread the vision of the mission of the church.	Starter Entrepre-neur Pioneer	
Artistic Expression	..have a special ability to communicate God's message through the fine arts, including drama, creative writing, music, and drawing. Through their God-given creativity, they use their gifts to draw others in and focus on God, His creation, and His message.	Expressive Innovative Creative	
Craftsmanship	..are uniquely skilled at working with raw materials, helping to create things that are used for ministry or that help meet tangible needs. They can be found fixing, remodeling, and sprucing up buildings, and/or creating and stitching items--honoring God and benefitting His people in practical ways.	Skilled Creative Resourceful	
Discernment	..distinguish between good and evil, truth and error, right and wrong. These people provide much-needed insight, point out inconsistencies in the teaching of God's Word, challenge deceitfulness in others, help sort out impure motives from pure ones, and identify spiritual warfare.	Intuitive Perceptive Sensitive	

YOUR UNIQUE DESIGN

Gift	Brief Definition Those with gifts of..	Description	Someone with Gift:
Evangelism	..seem to be always seeking to build meaningful relationships with non-believers and are often able to steer conversations with these people to spiritual things. They communicate the good news of Jesus to unbelievers in such a way that they see people believe and commit to following Christ.	Forthright Influential Heart for the lost	
Exhortation	..offer a word of hope combined with a gentle push to action to those who are discouraged, tentative, or needing direction. People with this gift come alongside to offer reassurance and affirmation, and, when needed, to challenge or confront, all with the goal of seeing others grow to greater maturity in their faith.	Affirming Motivator Heartening	
Faith	..have that extra measure of confidence in God and His promises, helping inspire others to greater belief. Those with this gift live constantly in the knowledge that God works all things for their good and the good of others who are called according to His purposes.	Believing Hopeful Secure	
Giving	..have an extra measure of the ability to be generous. People with this gift live as if everything they have belongs to God, knowing that God will provide for their needs. Giving may involve money as well as other resources like housing, food, clothing, etc.	Resourceful Sacrificial Steward	
Helps	..meet the practical needs of others and of the church/organizations in order to enhance, support, or accomplish ministry. Indicators of someone with the gift of helps are that he/she serves willingly, cheerfully, humbly, and wherever needed.	Humble Available Depend-able	

THOSE WITH THE GIFT OF...

DISCERNMENT

DISTINGUISH BETWEEN GOOD AND EVIL, TRUTH AND ERROR, RIGHT AND WRONG. THESE PEOPLE PROVIDE MUCH-NEEDED INSIGHT, GUARDING THE BODY AGAINST FALSE TEACHING AND EVIL INFLUENCES.

EVANGELISM

FIND WAYS TO BUILD RELATIONSHIPS AND COMMUNICATE THE GOOD NEWS OF JESUS TO PEOPLE IN SUCH A WAY THAT THEY COMMIT TO FOLLOWING CHRIST.

EXHORTATION

OFFER A WORD OF HOPE TO THOSE WHO ARE DISCOURAGED OR NEEDING DIRECTION. THEY ENCOURAGE OTHERS TO GROW TO GREATER MATURITY IN THEIR FAITH.

FAITH

HAVE THAT EXTRA MEASURE OF CONFIDENCE IN GOD AND HIS PROMISES, HELPING INSPIRE OTHERS TO GREATER TRUST IN THE LORD.

GIVING

HAVE AN EXTRA MEASURE OF THE ABILITY TO BE GENEROUS. GIVING MAY INVOLVE MONEY AS WELL AS OTHER RESOURCES LIKE HOUSING, FOOD, CLOTHING, ETC.

HELPS

MEET THE PRACTICAL NEEDS OF OTHERS AND OF THE CHURCH OR ORGANIZATIONS IN ORDER TO HELP ACCOMPLISH MINISTRY. THEY SERVE CHEERFULLY AND HUMBLY WHEREVER NEEDED.

HOSPITALITY

HAVE THE DIVINE ABILITY TO MAKE PEOPLE FEEL WELCOME AND ACCEPTED—PERHAPS IN THEIR HOME OR IN THE CHURCH. THEY CREATE AN ATMOSPHERE WHERE RELATIONSHIPS AND COMMUNITY CAN FLOURISH.

YOUR UNIQUE DESIGN: GUIDE

CLASS GUIDE

Gift	Brief Definition Those with gifts of...	Description	Someone with Gift:
Hospitality	...have the divine ability to make people feel welcome and accepted–anywhere at any time. People with this gift enjoy connecting people with each other and creating an atmosphere where relationships and community can flourish.	Accepting Welcoming Friendly	
Intercession	...feel compelled by God to pray on a daily basis for others. They are completely convinced of the awesome power and necessity of prayer. They pray as a first response to any given situation, during that situation, and afterwards.	Faithful Trusting Aware	
Knowledge	...bring Biblical truth and God-given insight to the church. They may also receive a word from God that is uniquely timed and tailored for a given situation. People with the gift of knowledge may also be those who have a keen desire to study and know God's Word, and God may use this understanding of Scripture to speak a word of knowledge to a person or group.	Aware Perceptive Student of Scripture	
Leadership	...are visionary, good motivators, and effective directors–helping inspire others to achieve God's purpose. Leadership involves not only having a vision of the preferred future for the church or an organization, but also having clarity on next steps to achieve that vision, the ability to communicate vision in a way that inspires others, and equip the rest of the team to pursue the same direction together.	Visionary Goal-oriented Credible	
Mercy	...provide comfort, support, and presence to those who are suffering, in crisis, or otherwise hurting. Those with this gift reach out to others who are broken. They show God's heart to those who need the empathy of a listening ear.	Caring Compassionate Kind	

YOUR UNIQUE DESIGN

Gift	Brief Definition Those with gifts of...	Description	Someone with Gift:
Prophecy	...have the gift that God uses to convict His people of sin and their need for repentance. Prophecy brings warning, challenge, correction, and confrontation without compromise.	Exposes Challenges Bold	
Shepherding	...provide nurture and guidance to others so that they grow in spiritual maturity and Christ-like character. People with the shepherding gift seek to walk alongside someone for a long or short season and direct them to Jesus and His offer of life, hope, and peace.	Fosters health Guide Counselor	
Teaching	...study, understand, explain, and apply Scripture's truths in such a way that people grow in their own understanding, are challenged, and are inspired to apply what they've learned. This can be done in a church or other context, since God's truth is true everywhere.	Communicator Inspiring Applies learning	
Wisdom	...use their God-given insight and information by applying it to specific situations, providing guidance in the church. They see the right course of action in the midst of otherwise confusing or overwhelming circumstances. Input from those with wisdom can shift a group's direction or help guide someone toward greater clarity.	Guide Perceptive Good judgment	
Healing	...follow the pattern we see in the life and ministry of Jesus where healing was physical, mental, emotional, and/or spiritual. Often also used by God to authenticate a message or a ministry. Always it is to show God's grace and mercy and power.	Restorer Responsive Intercessor	

THOSE WITH THE GIFT OF...

INTERCESSION
FEEL COMPELLED BY GOD TO PRAY OFTEN FOR OTHERS. THEY ARE CONVICTED OF THE AWESOME POWER AND NECESSITY OF PRAYER. PRAYER IS THEIR FIRST RESPONSE TO ANY SITUATION.

KNOWLEDGE
BRING BIBLICAL TRUTH AND GOD-GIVEN INSIGHT TO THE CHURCH. THEY MAY ALSO RECEIVE A SPECIAL WORD FROM GOD FOR A GIVEN SITUATION. THEY GIVE INSIGHTS AND INFORMATION THAT BRING THE BODY TO A PLACE OF GREATER UNDERSTANDING.

LEADERSHIP
HELP INSPIRE OTHERS TO ACHIEVE GOD'S PURPOSE. LEADERSHIP INVOLVES NOT ONLY HAVING A VISION FOR THE CHURCH OR AN ORGANIZATION, BUT ALSO HAVING CLARITY ON THE PATH TO ACHIEVE IT, THE ABILITY TO COMMUNICATE IT, AND THE ABILITY TO EQUIP THE REST OF THE TEAM TO PURSUE IT TOGETHER.

MERCY
PROVIDE COMFORT, SUPPORT, AND PRESENCE TO THOSE WHO ARE SUFFERING, IN CRISIS, OR OTHERWISE HURTING. THEY REACH OUT AND SHOW GOD'S HEART TO OTHERS WHO ARE BROKEN.

PROPHECY
ARE USED BY GOD TO CONVICT HIS PEOPLE OF SIN AND THEIR NEED FOR REPENTANCE. PROPHECY IS ABOUT WARNING, CHALLENGE, CORRECTION, AND SOMETIMES CONFRONTATION.

SHEPHERDING
COME ALONGSIDE OTHERS TO PROVIDE NURTURE AND GUIDANCE SO THAT OTHERS GROW IN SPIRITUAL MATURITY AND CHRIST-LIKE CHARACTER. THIS CAN BE IN A GROUP SETTING OR A ONE-ON-ONE RELATIONSHIP.

YOUR UNIQUE DESIGN

Gift	Brief Definition Those with gifts of...	Description	Someone with Gift
Prophecy	...have the gift that God uses to convict His people of sin and their need for repentance. Prophecy brings warning, challenge, correction, and confrontation without compromise.	Exposes Challenges Bold	
Shepherding	...provide nurture and guidance to others so that they grow in spiritual maturity and Christ-like character. People with the shepherding gift seek to walk alongside someone for a long or short season and direct them to Jesus and His offer of life, hope, and peace.	Fosters health Guide Counselor	
Teaching	...study, understand, explain, and apply Scripture's truths in such a way that people grow in their own understanding, are challenged, and are inspired to apply what they've learned. This can be done in a church or other context, since God's truth is true everywhere.	Communicator Inspiring Applies learning	
Wisdom	...use their God-given insight and information by applying it to specific situations, providing guidance in the church. They see the right course of action in the midst of otherwise confusing or overwhelming circumstances. Input from those with wisdom can shift a group's direction or help guide someone toward greater clarity.	Guide Perceptive Good judgment	
Healing	...follow the pattern we see in the life and ministry of Jesus where healing was physical, mental, emotional and/or spiritual. Often also used by God to authenticate a message or a ministry. Always it is to show God's grace and mercy and power.	Restorer Responsive Intercessor	

CLASS GUIDE

Gift	Brief Definition Those with gifts of...	Description	Someone with Gift
Miraculous Powers	...help authenticate a ministry, encourages a body of believers, and show the power of God in the life and ministry of Jesus. His miracles included feeding the multitudes, turning water into wine, raising the dead and walking on water.	Responsive Courageous Alert	
Tongues	...may speak in other languages as the Spirit enables them (Acts 2), may speak in an unknown language (that of "angels"- 1 Cor 13), may speak to God in tongues (1 Cor 13). It can also be a way of "uttering the mysteries of the Spirit," and "sounding a clear call" to God's people (1 Cor 14). Usually accompanied by the Interpretation of Tongues gift.	Responsive Expressive Worshipful	
Interpretation of Tongues	...help the rest of the Body of Christ understand the message being spoken by those with the gift of Tongues. May be given concurrently to someone with Tongues.	Responsive Obedient Discerning	

THOSE WITH THE GIFT OF...

TEACHING

STUDY, UNDERSTAND, EXPLAIN, AND APPLY SCRIPTURE'S TRUTHS IN SUCH A WAY THAT PEOPLE GROW IN THEIR OWN UNDERSTANDING, ARE CHALLENGED, AND ARE INSPIRED TO APPLY WHAT THEY'VE LEARNED. THIS CAN BE IN A CHURCH OR OTHER CONTEXT.

WISDOM

ARE GIFTED BY GOD TO SEE THE RIGHT COURSE OF ACTION IN THE MIDST OF DIFFICULT SITUATIONS. THE WISE GUIDANCE CAN BE TO HELP A GROUP OR AN INDIVIDUAL.

BEFORE WE COVER THE LAST 4 GIFTS, WHICH ARE IN A SOMEWHAT DIFFERENT CATEGORY, ARE THERE ANY QUESTIONS ABOUT THE DEFINITIONS I JUST GAVE?

[Don't spend too much time here, as we cover FAQs next session!!]

THESE LAST FOUR ARE IN DARKER-SHADED BOXES FOR SEVERAL REASONS:

--IN AN ASSESSMENT LIKE THIS, IT'S DIFFICULT TO PROVIDE THREE QUESTIONS FOR THESE FOUR GIFTS THAT CUT ACROSS MOST PEOPLE'S EXPERIENCE OF THE GIFT. SO, YOU MAY IN FACT HAVE ONE OF THESE GIFTS, BUT YOUR SCORE WAS LOW.

--YOU MAY ALSO HAVE NEVER HAD THE OPPORTUNITY TO SEE IF YOU HAVE ONE OF THESE GIFTS, SO YOUR SCORE WOULD LIKELY HAVE BEEN A ZERO. THAT MAY NOT MEAN YOU DON'T HAVE THE GIFT.

--SOME CHURCHES HAVE LOTS OF CONFUSION ABOUT USE OF THESE FOUR GIFTS. SOME CHURCHES TAKE THE POSITION THAT GOD DOESN'T GRANT THESE GIFTS ANYMORE...SO, YOUR OWN CHURCH HISTORY CAN IMPACT YOUR SCORE AS WELL.

YOUR UNIQUE DESIGN

Gift	Brief Definition Those with gifts of...	Description	Someone with Gift:
Prophecy	...have the gift that God uses to convict His people of sin and their need for repentance. Prophecy brings warning, challenge, correction, and confrontation without compromise.	Exposes Challenges Bold	
Shepherding	...provide nurture and guidance to others so that they grow in spiritual maturity and Christ-like character. People with the shepherding gift seek to walk alongside someone for a long or short season and direct them to Jesus and His offer of life, hope, and peace.	Fosters health Guide Counselor	
Teaching	...study, understand, explain, and apply Scripture's truths in such a way that people grow in their own understanding, are challenged, and are inspired to apply what they've learned. This can be done in a church or other context, since God's truth is true everywhere.	Communicator Inspiring Applies learning	
Wisdom	...use their God-given insight and information by applying it to specific situations, providing guidance in the church. They see the right course of action in the midst of otherwise confusing or overwhelming circumstances. Input from those with wisdom can shift a group's direction or help guide someone toward greater clarity.	Guide Perceptive Good judgment	
Healing	...follow the pattern we see in the life and ministry of Jesus where healing was physical, mental, emotional, and/or spiritual. Often also used by God to authenticate a message or a ministry. Always it is to show God's grace and mercy and power.	Restorer Responsive Intercessor	

CLASS GUIDE

Gift	Brief Definition Those with gifts of...	Description	Someone with Gift
Miraculous Powers	...help authenticate a ministry, encourage a body of believers, and show the power of God in the life and ministry of Jesus. His miracles included feeding the multitudes, turning water into wine, raising the dead, and walking on water.	Responsive Courageous Alert	
Tongues	...may speak in other languages as the Spirit enables them (Acts 2), may speak in an unknown language (that of "angels"-1 Cor. 13), may speak to God in tongues (1 Cor. 13). It can also be a way of "uttering the mysteries of the Spirit," and "sounding a clear call" to God's people (1 Cor. 14). Usually accompanied by the Interpretation of Tongues gift.	Responsive Expressive Worshipful	
Interpretation of Tongues	...help the rest of the Body of Christ understand the message being spoken by those with the gift of Tongues. May be given concurrently to someone with Tongues.	Responsive Obedient Discerning	

THOSE WITH THE GIFT OF...

HEALING

THE GIFT OF HEALING FOLLOWS THE PATTERN WE SEE IN THE MINISTRY OF JESUS WHERE HEALING WAS PHYSICAL, MENTAL, EMOTIONAL, AND/OR SPIRITUAL. OFTEN IN SCRIPTURE HEALING IS USED BY GOD TO AUTHENTICATE A MESSAGE OR A MINISTRY. ALWAYS IT IS TO SHOW GOD'S MERCY AND GRACE AND POWER. SOMETIMES HEALING IS INSTANT AND SOMETIMES IT HAPPENS OVER TIME. OUR GOD IS A GOD OF RESTORATION AND WHOLENESS, AND HEALING IS ONE WAY IN WHICH WE SEE THAT.

MIRACULOUS POWERS

MIRACULOUS POWERS (THE ABILITY TO PERFORM MIRACLES) ARE GIVEN TO INDIVIDUALS IN THE BODY OF CHRIST TO AUTHENTICATE A MINISTRY, ENCOURAGE A BODY OF BELIEVERS, AND TO SHOW THE POWER OF GOD. IN THE LIFE OF JESUS, THIS INCLUDED WALKING ON WATER, TURNING WATER INTO WINE, AND FEEDING 5000 PEOPLE FROM FIVE LOAVES AND TWO FISH. IN ACTS 19:11-12 WE READ: "GOD DID EXTRAORDINARY MIRACLES THROUGH PAUL, SO THAT EVEN HANDKERCHIEFS AND APRONS THAT HAD TOUCHED HIM WERE TAKEN TO THE SICK, AND THEIR ILLNESSES WERE CURED AND THE EVIL SPIRITS LEFT THEM."

TONGUES

THOSE WITH THE GIFT OF TONGUES MAY SPEAK IN OTHER LANGUAGES AS THE SPIRIT ENABLES THEM (ACTS 2) OR MAY SPEAK IN AN UNKNOWN LANGUAGE (THAT OF "ANGELS"-1 CORINTHIANS 13:1); MAY SPEAK TO GOD IN TONGUES (1 CORINTHIANS 14:2). SCRIPTURE SAYS IN ADDITION TO TONGUES BEING OTHER LANGUAGES IT IS ALSO A WAY OF UTTERING "MYSTERIES BY THE SPIRIT" (1 CORINTHIANS 14:2). TO BE UNDERSTOOD BY THE BODY, TONGUES MUST BE ACCOMPANIED BY THE GIFT OF INTERPRETATION OF TONGUES. THIS CAN BE IN THE SETTING OF WORSHIP OR OF PRAYER.

INTERPRETATION OF TONGUES

HELP THE REST OF THE BODY OF CHRIST UNDERSTAND THE MESSAGE BEING SPOKEN BY THOSE WITH THE GIFT OF TONGUES. A PERSON WITH THE GIFT OF TONGUES MAY ALSO BE GIVEN THE GIFT TO INTERPRET.

[Pause here to see if there are questions or areas that need clarification (keeping in mind that you need to leave time for small group discussion AND that we will take on key FAQs NEXT session).]

Sharing Gifts Discovered

- Share your **top results**.
- What were **confirmations** of what you already knew?
- What were **surprises**?
- Any **disappointments**?
- Share your lowest scoring one(s)--**what was NOT a gift for you?**

Listing Gifts

Individual Exercise--Homework

YOUR UNIQUE DESIGN

Group Exercise

REPORTING ON SPIRITUAL GIFTS DISCOVERED

SHARE YOUR TOP RESULTS

WHAT WERE CONFIRMATIONS OF WHAT YOU ALREADY KNEW?

WHAT WERE SURPRISES? (WHAT SHOWED UP ON YOUR LIST THAT YOU DIDN'T EXPECT? WHAT DIDN'T SHOW UP THAT YOU THOUGHT WAS AN AREA OF GIFTEDNESS?)

ANY DISAPPOINTMENTS? (ARE YOU DISAPPOINTED WITH YOUR LIST OF GIFTS IN SOME WAY?)

SHARE YOUR LOWEST SCORING ONE(S) - WHAT WAS NOT A GIFT FOR YOU?

JOT DOWN ONE OR TWO THINGS YOU WANT TO REMEMBER FROM THIS SESSION--ABOUT YOUR UNIQUENESS, GOD'S CALL, YOUR BEING SET APART, BEING EQUIPPED, ABOUT THE BODY OF CHRIST...WHATEVER GOD BRINGS TO MIND.

READ 1 CORINTHIANS 12.

CLASS GUIDE

HomeWork

Complete the FINDING GIFTS exercise below (Est time 10-15 minutes)

1. FOR THE FOLLOWING THREE PASSAGES, CIRCLE THE ACTIVITIES YOU NOTE AND JOT DOWN A POSSIBLE THEME THAT YOU SEE IN ALL THREE:

Praise him with the sounding of the trumpet, praise him with the harp and lyre, praise him with timbrel and dancing, praise him with strings and pipe, praise him with the clash of cymbals, praise him with resounding cymbals. (Psalm 150:3-5).

Then Miriam the prophet, Aaron's sister, took a timbrel in her hand, and all the women followed her, with timbrels and dancing. Miriam sang to them: "Sing to the Lord, for he is highly exalted. Both horse and driver he has hurled into the sea" (Exodus 15:20-21).

Wearing a linen ephod, David was dancing before the Lord with all his might, while he and Israel were bringing up the ark of the Lord with shouts and the sound of trumpets. (2 Samuel 6:14-15).

2. FOR THE FOLLOWING THREE PASSAGES, WHAT IS THE GIFT MENTIONED OR IMPLIED?

Epaphras, who is one of you and a servant of Christ Jesus, sends greetings. He is always wrestling in prayer for you, that you may stand firm in all the will of God, mature and fully assured (Colossians 4:12).

I have not stopped giving thanks for you, remembering you in my prayers (Ephesians 1:16).

I thank God, whom I serve, as my ancestors did, with a clear conscience, as night and day, I constantly remember you in my prayers (2 Timothy 1:3).

3. CIRCLE THE SPIRITUAL GIFTS MENTIONED OR IMPLIED IN EACH OF THE FOLLOWING PASSAGES.

Now the Lord spoke to Moses, saying, "See, I have called by name Bezalel, the son of Uri, the son of Hur, of the tribe of Judah. I have filled him with the Spirit of God in wisdom, in understanding, in knowledge, and in all kinds of craftsmanship, to make artistic designs for work in gold, in silver, and in bronze, and in the cutting of stones for settings, and in the carving of wood, that he may work in all kinds of craftsmanship (Exodus 31:1-5, NASB)

Now to each one the manifestation of the Spirit is given for the common good. To one there is given through the Spirit a message of wisdom, to another a message of knowledge by means of the same Spirit, to another faith by the same Spirit, to another gifts of healing by that one Spirit, to another miraculous powers, to another prophecy; to another distinguishing between spirits,

HOPE WHAT STAYS WITH YOU IS NOT JUST WHAT WERE YOUR GIFTS BUT WHAT GIFTS OF OTHERS YOU IDENTIFIED.

RECOGNIZE YOUR ROLE IS TO CALL OUT AND AFFIRM THE GIFTS WE SEE IN ONE ANOTHER.

SMALL GROUP EXERCISE—BRIEF REPORTING ON SPIRITUAL GIFTS DISCOVERED.

IN GROUPS AT YOUR TABLES, DISCUSS THE QUESTIONS ON THIS SLIDE...MAKE SURE TO ALLOW EACH PERSON TIME TO SHARE THEIR RESULTS AND REACTIONS.

- SHARE YOUR TOP 3 GIFTS.
- WHAT WERE CONFIRMATIONS OF WHAT YOU ALREADY KNEW? (AFFIRMATIONS?)
- WHAT WERE SURPRISES? (WHAT SHOWED UP ON YOUR LIST THAT YOU DIDN'T EXPECT? OR, WHAT DIDN'T SHOW UP THAT YOU EXPECTED?)
- ANY DISAPPOINTMENTS? (ARE YOU DISAPPOINTED WITH YOUR LIST OF GIFTS?)
- SHARE YOUR LOWEST SCORING ONE(S)--WHAT WAS NOT A GIFT FOR YOU?

WE'LL DO MORE GIFT-DEBRIEFING NEXT WEEK AS WELL.

TAKE A MOMENT NOW TO JOT DOWN ONE OR TWO THINGS YOU WANT TO REMEMBER FROM THIS SESSION.

IF YOU'RE SO INCLINED, BETWEEN NOW AND NEXT WEEK, DO THE LISTING GIFTS EXERCISE IN YOUR BOOK:

LISTING GIFTS (INDIVIDUAL EXERCISE) ON P. 19-20 IN YOUR WORKBOOK.

AS YOU READ THE TWO PAGES, UNDERLINE OR CIRCLE ALL THE GIFTS NAMED OR IMPLIED. LIKELY WILL TAKE YOU 10-15 MINUTES TO COMPLETE.

[Note: This is Appendix D in your Facilitator's Guide.]

AND, BETWEEN NOW AND NEXT WEEK, PLEASE READ 1 CORINTHIANS 12. WE ALSO HAVE A TABLE OF RESOURCES FOR YOU. PLEASE FEEL FREE TO PERUSE THOSE THIS WEEK OR NEXT.

LET'S CLOSE IN PRAYER. PRAY.

YOUR UNIQUE DESIGN CLASS FACILITATOR SCRIPTS
SESSION 2: RECOGNIZING AND AFFIRMING GIFTS

Preparation/Set-up

Need:

- Projector or TV/Monitor
- Screen
- HDMI connector and cable
- Laptop with class slides
- Backup USB w/slides
- Microphone/sound system
- Remote control for laptop with back-up batteries and USB connector
- Pens
- Your Unique Design Class Guide books—one per participant.
- Bags of supplies for the mini-Passion exercise (magazines with lots of photos, construction paper, markers, crayons, yarn, tape, glue-stick, clay, Playdoh, Legos, chenille sticks/pipe-cleaners, etc.) Pretty much anything can work for this exercise.
- Table of resources, if providing (might include lists of serving opportunities, recommended books, next steps, etc.)

Classroom set-up: Music stand or podium for scripts, projection screen, cart for laptop and projector, or laptop connected to a TV, Your Unique Design workbooks—one for each participant, round tables (or rectangular, if round not available in the room you plan to use) with seats for 4-6 at each table, a table for any additional resources and name tags, a table for cups/plates/water/goodies (if you have a plan to ask people to provide such), coffee/tea cart.

Prior to class:
- Put pens on tables
- Put one bag of supplies for mini-Passion exercise on each table

Note: take time to manually add page numbers throughout script, based on the latest version of the workbook provided to participants.

Spiritual Gifts are

- ☐ Special abilities
- ☐ Distributed by God according to His choosing, His grace, His mercy
- ☐ through His Holy Spirit
- ☐ to each and every believer in Jesus
- ☐ in order to be used to glorify God
- ☐ and for the common good and strengthening of the Body of Christ

---

1 Corinthians 12:12-30

12 Just as a body, though one, has many parts, but all its many parts form one body, so it is with Christ. 13 For we were all baptized by one Spirit so as to form one body—whether Jews or Gentiles, slave or free—and we were all given the one Spirit to drink. 14 Even so the body is not made up of one part but of many. 15 Now if the foot should say, "Because I am not a hand, I do not belong to the body," it would not for that reason stop being part of the body. 16 And if the ear should say, "Because I am not an eye, I do not belong to the body," it would not for that reason stop being part of the body. 17 If the whole body were an eye, where would the sense of hearing be? If the whole body were an ear, where would the sense of smell be? 18 But in fact God has placed the parts in the body, every one of them, just as he wanted them to be. 19 If they were all one part, where would the body be? 20 As it is, there are many parts, but one body.

CLASS GUIDE

Session 2
Recognizing and Affirming Gifts

Body of Christ

CONTEXT OF THE CHURCH AS THE BODY OF CHRIST

1 CORINTHIANS 12:12-30 | Just as a body, though one, has many parts, but all its many parts form one body so it is with Christ. For we were all baptized by one Spirit so as to form one body—whether Jews or Gentiles, slave or free—and we were all given the one Spirit to drink. Even so the body is not made up of one part but of many.

Now if the foot should say, "Because I am not a hand, I do not belong to the body," it would not for that reason stop being part of the body. And if the ear should say, "Because I am not an eye, I do not belong to the body," it would not for that reason stop being part of the body. If the whole body were an eye, where would the sense of hearing be? If the whole body were an ear, where would the sense of smell be? But in fact God has placed the parts in the body, every one of them, just as he wanted them to be. If they were all one part, where would the body be? As it is, there are many parts, but one body.

The eye cannot say to the hand, "I don't need you!" And the head cannot say to the feet, "I don't need you!" On the contrary, those parts of the body that seem to be weaker are indispensable, and the parts that we think are less honorable we treat with special honor. And the parts that are unpresentable are treated with special modesty, while our presentable parts need no special treatment. But God has put the body together, giving greater honor to the parts that lacked it, so that there should be no division in the body, but that its parts should have equal concern for each other. If one part suffers, every part suffers with it; if one part is honored, every part rejoices with it.

Now you are the body of Christ, and each one of you is a part of it. And God has placed in the church first of all apostles, second prophets, third teachers, then miracles, then gifts of healing, of helping, of guidance, and of different kinds of tongues. Are all apostles? Are all prophets? Are all teachers? Do all work miracles? Do all have gifts of healing? Do all speak in tongues? Do all interpret?

WAYS IN WHICH THE BODY ANALOGY APPLIES TO THE CHURCH:

SESSION 2

PRAY

REVIEW HIGHLIGHTS FROM LAST TIME:

- YOU ARE UNIQUE...CREATED UNIQUELY AND SPECIALLY BY GOD.
- YOU ARE CALLED...CHOSEN...SET APART.
- GOD SAYS HIS PLAN INVOLVES YOU AND HE WILL EQUIP YOU TO BE ABLE TO DO WHAT HE ASKS YOU TO DO.
- AND A PIECE OF THAT EQUIPMENT IS SPIRITUAL GIFTS.

OUR WORKING DEFINITION OF SPIRITUAL GIFTS IS:

- SPECIAL ABILITIES.
- GIVEN/DISTRIBUTED BY GOD ACCORDING TO HIS CHOOSING, HIS GRACE, HIS MERCY.
- THROUGH HOLY SPIRIT.
- TO EACH AND EVERY BELIEVER IN JESUS.
- IN ORDER TO BE USED TO GLORIFY GOD (1 PETER 4:11).
- AND FOR THE COMMON GOOD AND STRENGTHENING OF THE BODY OF CHRIST (EPH. 4:11-13).

LET'S ADD SOME MORE FOUNDATIONAL CONCEPTS:

CONTEXT OF THE CHURCH AS THE BODY OF CHRIST

1 CORINTHIANS 12:12-30 [analogy of the human body] [read these verses aloud]

AS I READ, UNDERLINE EACH REFERENCE TO "BODY," "ONE," "WHOLE."

JUST AS A BODY, THOUGH ONE, HAS MANY PARTS, BUT ALL ITS MANY PARTS FORM ONE BODY, SO IT IS WITH CHRIST. FOR WE WERE ALL BAPTIZED BY ONE SPIRIT SO AS TO FORM ONE BODY—WHETHER JEWS OR GENTILES, SLAVE OR FREE—AND WE WERE ALL GIVEN THE ONE SPIRIT TO DRINK. EVEN SO THE BODY IS NOT MADE UP OF ONE PART BUT OF MANY.

21 The eye cannot say to the hand, "I don't need you!" And the head cannot say to the feet, "I don't need you!" 22 On the contrary, those parts of the body that seem to be weaker are indispensable, 23 and the parts that we think are less honorable we treat with special honor. And the parts that are unpresentable are treated with special modesty, 24 while our presentable parts need no special treatment. But God has put the body together, giving greater honor to the parts that lacked it, 25 so that there should be no division in the body, but that its parts should have equal concern for each other. 26 If one part suffers, every part suffers with it; if one part is honored, every part rejoices with it.

27 Now you are the body of Christ, and each one of you is a part of it. 28 And God has placed in the church first of all apostles, second prophets, third teachers, then miracles, then gifts of healing, of helping, of guidance, and of different kinds of tongues. 29 Are all apostles? Are all prophets? Are all teachers? Do all work miracles? 30 Do all have gifts of healing? Do all speak in tongues? Do all interpret?

Session 2
Recognizing and Affirming Gifts

Body of Christ

CONTEXT OF THE CHURCH AS THE BODY OF CHRIST

1 CORINTHIANS 12:12-30 | Just as a body, though one, has many parts, but all its many parts form one body so it is with Christ. For we were all baptized by one Spirit so as to form one body—whether Jews or Gentiles, slave or free—and we were all given the one Spirit to drink. Even so the body is not made up of one part but of many.

Now if the foot should say, "Because I am not a hand, I do not belong to the body," it would not for that reason stop being part of the body. And if the ear should say, "Because I am not an eye, I do not belong to the body," it would not for that reason stop being part of the body. If the whole body were an eye, where would the sense of hearing be? If the whole body were an ear, where would the sense of smell be? But in fact God has placed the parts in the body, every one of them, just as he wanted them to be. If they were all one part, where would the body be? As it is, there are many parts, but one body.

The eye cannot say to the hand, "I don't need you!" And the head cannot say to the feet, "I don't need you!" On the contrary, those parts of the body that seem to be weaker are indispensable, and the parts that we think are less honorable we treat with special honor. And the parts that are unpresentable are treated with special modesty, while our presentable parts need no special treatment. But God has put the body together, giving greater honor to the parts that lacked it, so that there should be no division in the body, but that its parts should have equal concern for each other. If one part suffers, every part suffers with it; if one part is honored, every part rejoices with it.

Now you are the body of Christ, and each one of you is a part of it. And God has placed in the church first of all apostles, second prophets, third teachers, then miracles, then gifts of healing, of helping, of guidance, and of different kinds of tongues. Are all apostles? Are all prophets? Are all teachers? Do all work miracles? Do all have gifts of healing? Do all speak in tongues? Do all interpret?

WAYS IN WHICH THE BODY ANALOGY APPLIES TO THE CHURCH:

NOW IF THE FOOT SHOULD SAY, "BECAUSE I AM NOT A HAND, I DO NOT BELONG TO THE BODY," IT WOULD NOT FOR THAT REASON STOP BEING PART OF THE BODY. AND IF THE EAR SHOULD SAY, "BECAUSE I AM NOT AN EYE, I DO NOT BELONG TO THE BODY," IT WOULD NOT FOR THAT REASON STOP BEING PART OF THE BODY. IF THE WHOLE BODY WERE AN EYE, WHERE WOULD THE SENSE OF HEARING BE? IF THE WHOLE BODY WERE AN EAR, WHERE WOULD THE SENSE OF SMELL BE? BUT IN FACT GOD HAS PLACED THE PARTS IN THE BODY, EVERY ONE OF THEM, JUST AS HE WANTED THEM TO BE. IF THEY WERE ALL ONE PART, WHERE WOULD THE BODY BE? AS IT IS, THERE ARE MANY PARTS, BUT ONE BODY.

[Next Slide]

THE EYE CANNOT SAY TO THE HAND, "I DON'T NEED YOU!" AND THE HEAD CANNOT SAY TO THE FEET, "I DON'T NEED YOU!" ON THE CONTRARY, THOSE PARTS OF THE BODY THAT SEEM TO BE WEAKER ARE INDISPENSABLE, AND THE PARTS THAT WE THINK ARE LESS HONORABLE WE TREAT WITH SPECIAL HONOR. AND THE PARTS THAT ARE UNPRESENTABLE ARE TREATED WITH SPECIAL MODESTY, WHILE OUR PRESENTABLE PARTS NEED NO SPECIAL TREATMENT. BUT GOD HAS PUT THE BODY TOGETHER, GIVING GREATER HONOR TO THE PARTS THAT LACKED IT, SO THAT THERE SHOULD BE NO DIVISION IN THE BODY, BUT THAT ITS PARTS SHOULD HAVE EQUAL CONCERN FOR EACH OTHER. IF ONE PART SUFFERS, EVERY PART SUFFERS WITH IT; IF ONE PART IS HONORED, EVERY PART REJOICES WITH IT.

[Next Slide]

NOW YOU ARE THE BODY OF CHRIST, AND EACH ONE OF YOU IS A PART OF IT. AND GOD HAS PLACED IN THE CHURCH FIRST OF ALL APOSTLES, SECOND PROPHETS, THIRD TEACHERS, THEN MIRACLES, THEN GIFTS OF HEALING, OF HELPING, OF GUIDANCE, AND OF DIFFERENT KINDS OF TONGUES. ARE ALL APOSTLES? ARE ALL PROPHETS? ARE ALL TEACHERS? DO ALL WORK MIRACLES? DO ALL HAVE GIFTS OF HEALING? DO ALL SPEAK IN TONGUES? DO ALL INTERPRET?

[Ask the class to suggest some ways in which the Body analogy applies to the church, based on 1 Corinthians 12 -- responses may include: many parts/one Body; all belong; all indispensable; all to be honored; God's design; unity; concern for each other...]

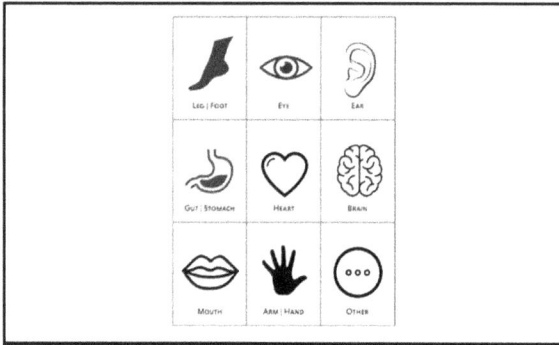

YOUR UNIQUE DESIGN

Group Exercise

BODY PARTS ACTIVITY—WHAT PART OF THE BODY ARE YOU?

TAKE A MOMENT OF SILENCE TO REFLECT ON WHAT YOU BRING TO THIS BODY OF CHRIST. THINK IN TERMS OF THE PARTS OF THE HUMAN BODY AND THEIR FUNCTIONS. THE GRAPHIC BELOW MAY BE USEFUL.

LEG | FOOT	EYE	EAR
GUT | STOMACH	HEART	BRAIN
MOUTH	ARM | HAND	OTHER

SHARE YOUR CHOICE WITH OTHERS AT YOUR TABLE.

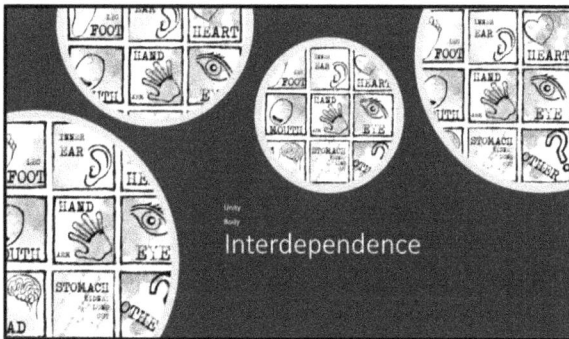

Interdependence

Love

Serving with love

INTERDEPENDENCE

Diversity | Unity:

Group Exercise

LOVE

AT YOUR TABLES, READ TOGETHER 1 CORINTHIANS 13:1-8. DISCUSS WHAT STANDS OUT TO YOU, KEEPING IN MIND THE CONTEXT WAS UNDERSTANDING AND LIVING INTO USE OF SPIRITUAL GIFTS.

1 CORINTHIANS 13:1-8 | IF I SPEAK IN THE TONGUES OF MEN OR OF ANGELS, BUT DO NOT HAVE LOVE, I AM ONLY A RESOUNDING GONG OR A CLANGING CYMBAL. IF I HAVE THE GIFT OF PROPHECY AND CAN FATHOM ALL MYSTERIES AND ALL KNOWLEDGE, AND IF I HAVE A FAITH THAT CAN MOVE MOUNTAINS, BUT DO NOT HAVE LOVE, I AM NOTHING. IF I GIVE ALL I POSSESS TO THE POOR AND GIVE OVER MY BODY TO HARDSHIP THAT I MAY BOAST, BUT DO NOT HAVE LOVE, I GAIN NOTHING.

LOVE IS PATIENT, LOVE IS KIND. IT DOES NOT ENVY, IT DOES NOT BOAST, IT IS NOT PROUD. IT DOES NOT DISHONOR OTHERS, IT IS NOT SELF-SEEKING, IT IS NOT EASILY ANGERED, IT KEEPS NO RECORD OF WRONGS. LOVE DOES NOT DELIGHT IN EVIL BUT REJOICES WITH THE TRUTH. IT ALWAYS PROTECTS, ALWAYS TRUSTS, ALWAYS HOPES, ALWAYS PERSEVERES.

LOVE NEVER FAILS.

23 GIFTS

Don't neglect.

Stewards.

Clarity.

Meaning and connection.

Church health.

LET'S TAKE A MOMENT TO DO FUN ACTIVITY TO HELP MAKE THIS POINT

BODY PARTS ACTIVITY

IN REFLECTING ON YOUR GIFTS ASSESSMENT RESULTS, WHAT PART OF THE BODY ARE YOU? EYES? EARS? HANDS? FEET? MAYBE AN INVISIBLE, BUT ESSENTIAL ORGAN LIKE THE PANCREAS OR THYROID?

ARE YOU MORE THINKING, FEELING, DOING, SENSING, LISTENING, SPEAKING, PROCESSING? GUT? HEART? ARMS? LEGS? HEAD? MOUTH?

TAKE A MOMENT OF SILENCE TO REFLECT ON WHAT YOU BRING TO THIS BODY OF CHRIST. THINK IN TERMS OF THE PARTS OF THE HUMAN BODY AND THEIR FUNCTIONS. THE GRAPHIC ON P. 24 OF YOUR BOOKLET MAY BE USEFUL.

NOW—SHARE WITH YOUR TABLE WHY YOU CHOSE THAT REGION OF THE BODY...

GUT MIGHT MEAN DISCERNMENT? SPEAKING MIGHT MEAN TEACHING OR PROPHECY OR TONGUES? HEAD MIGHT BE WISDOM OR KNOWLEDGE? HEART MIGHT BE MERCY? HANDS MIGHT BE HOSPITALITY OR HELPS/SERVICE? FEET MIGHT BE EVANGELISM OR SHEPHERDING?

BUILDING ON OUR FOUNDATION:

INTERDEPENDENCE...GOD'S DESIGN FOR THE CHURCH IS AS A BODY
- SCRIPTURE SPEAKS OF GREAT DIVERSITY, BUT ALSO THAT UNITY SHOULD BE A HALLMARK OF THE BODY OF CHRIST.
- IT'S REALLY CLEAR THAT ALTHOUGH WE ARE UNIQUELY CREATED AND GIFTED WE ARE--WITH GOD'S HELP AND WITH GOD'S POWER--TO LIVE IN UNITY AND NOT DISUNITY.

SERVING WITH LOVE—CONTEXT OF USING GIFTS 1 CORINTHIANS: 12 - 13
- THEY WILL KNOW YOU ARE BELIEVERS BECAUSE OF YOUR GREAT PROGRAMS OR THEY WILL KNOW YOU ARE FOLLOWERS OF JESUS BECAUSE YOUR MINISTRY TEAMS ARE PHENOMENAL???

---

1 Corinthians 13:1-8

1 If I speak in the tongues of men or of angels, but do not have love, I am only a resounding gong or a clanging cymbal. 2 If I have the gift of prophecy and can fathom all mysteries and all knowledge, and if I have a faith that can move mountains, but do not have love, I am nothing. 3 If I give all I possess to the poor and give over my body to hardship that I may boast, but do not have love, I gain nothing.

4 Love is patient, love is kind. It does not envy, it does not boast, it is not proud. 5 It does not dishonor others, it is not self-seeking, it is not easily angered, it keeps no record of wrongs. 6 Love does not delight in evil but rejoices with the truth. 7 It always protects, always trusts, always hopes, always perseveres.

8 Love never fails. But where there are prophecies, they will cease; where there are tongues, they will be stilled; where there is knowledge, it will pass away.

INTERDEPENDENCE

Diversity | Unity:

Group Exercise

LOVE

AT YOUR TABLES, READ TOGETHER 1 CORINTHIANS 13:1-8. DISCUSS WHAT STANDS OUT TO YOU, KEEPING IN MIND THE CONTEXT WAS UNDERSTANDING AND LIVING INTO USE OF SPIRITUAL GIFTS.

1 CORINTHIANS 13:1-8 | IF I SPEAK IN THE TONGUES OF MEN OR OF ANGELS, BUT DO NOT HAVE LOVE, I AM ONLY A RESOUNDING GONG OR A CLANGING CYMBAL. IF I HAVE THE GIFT OF PROPHECY AND CAN FATHOM ALL MYSTERIES AND ALL KNOWLEDGE, AND IF I HAVE A FAITH THAT CAN MOVE MOUNTAINS, BUT DO NOT HAVE LOVE, I AM NOTHING. IF I GIVE ALL I POSSESS TO THE POOR AND GIVE OVER MY BODY TO HARDSHIP THAT I MAY BOAST, BUT DO NOT HAVE LOVE, I GAIN NOTHING.

LOVE IS PATIENT, LOVE IS KIND. IT DOES NOT ENVY, IT DOES NOT BOAST, IT IS NOT PROUD. IT DOES NOT DISHONOR OTHERS, IT IS NOT SELF-SEEKING, IT IS NOT EASILY ANGERED, IT KEEPS NO RECORD OF WRONGS. LOVE DOES NOT DELIGHT IN EVIL BUT REJOICES WITH THE TRUTH. IT ALWAYS PROTECTS, ALWAYS TRUSTS, ALWAYS HOPES, ALWAYS PERSEVERES.

LOVE NEVER FAILS.

23 GIFTS

| Don't neglect.
| Stewards.
| Clarity.
| Meaning and connection.
| Church health.

- No--what's the measure of how people will know you are a follower of Jesus? Love.
- Paul talks a lot about gifts in 1 Corinthians 12 and what's the very next chapter?
- Love.
- We use in weddings and that's not wrong but the context (Paul didn't write in chapters) is gifts. he goes straight from his tirade about using gifts correctly to the context has to be love or it has zero value—his message is very strong.

THIS IS A MAJOR THEME THROUGHOUT THE NEW TESTAMENT.

AT YOUR TABLES, READ TOGETHER 1 CORINTHIANS 13:1-8. DISCUSS WHAT STANDS OUT TO YOU, KEEPING IN MIND THE CONTEXT WAS UNDERSTANDING AND LIVING INTO USE OF SPIRITUAL GIFTS.

1 CORINTHIANS 13:1-8

1 If I speak in the tongues of men or of angels, but do not have love, I am only a resounding gong or a clanging cymbal. 2 If I have the gift of prophecy and can fathom all mysteries and all knowledge, and if I have a faith that can move mountains, but do not have love, I am nothing. 3 If I give all I possess to the poor and give over my body to hardship that I may boast, but do not have love, I gain nothing.

4 Love is patient, love is kind. It does not envy, it does not boast, it is not proud. 5 It does not dishonor others, it is not self-seeking, it is not easily angered, it keeps no record of wrongs. 6 Love does not delight in evil but rejoices with the truth. 7 It always protects, always trusts, always hopes, always perseveres.

8 Love never fails. But where there are prophecies, they will cease; where there are tongues, they will be stilled; where there is knowledge, it will pass away.

THESE ARE ALL KEY CONCEPTS IN UNDERSTANDING AND USING OUR GIFTS.

WHETHER OR NOT YOU DID THE LISTING GIFTS EXERCISE ON P. 19-20 IN YOUR WORKBOOK, IT'S IMPORTANT FOR ALL OF US TO HAVE A GOOD GRASP OF WHAT ARE GIFTS WE CAN FIND IN SCRIPTURE (AND WHAT ARE NOT)! WE ARE WORKING WITH A LIST OF 23 GIFTS THAT ARE MENTIONED OR IMPLIED IN THE BIBLE.

God's Word says, about gifts:

- Don't neglect
- Stewards
- Clarity
- Meaning and connection
- Health

HAND ARM

STOMACH KIDNEY LUNG GUT

HEART

FOOT LEG

Debriefing Gifts
FAQs

INTERDEPENDENCE

Diversity | Unity:

Group Exercise

Love

AT YOUR TABLES, READ TOGETHER 1 CORINTHIANS 13:1-8. DISCUSS WHAT STANDS OUT TO YOU, KEEPING IN MIND THE CONTEXT WAS UNDERSTANDING AND LIVING INTO USE OF SPIRITUAL GIFTS.

1 CORINTHIANS 13:1-8 | IF I SPEAK IN THE TONGUES OF MEN OR OF ANGELS, BUT DO NOT HAVE LOVE, I AM ONLY A RESOUNDING GONG OR A CLANGING CYMBAL. IF I HAVE THE GIFT OF PROPHECY AND CAN FATHOM ALL MYSTERIES AND ALL KNOWLEDGE, AND IF I HAVE A FAITH THAT CAN MOVE MOUNTAINS, BUT DO NOT HAVE LOVE, I AM NOTHING. IF I GIVE ALL I POSSESS TO THE POOR AND GIVE OVER MY BODY TO HARDSHIP THAT I MAY BOAST, BUT DO NOT HAVE LOVE, I GAIN NOTHING.

LOVE IS PATIENT, LOVE IS KIND. IT DOES NOT ENVY, IT DOES NOT BOAST, IT IS NOT PROUD. IT DOES NOT DISHONOR OTHERS, IT IS NOT SELF-SEEKING, IT IS NOT EASILY ANGERED, IT KEEPS NO RECORD OF WRONGS. LOVE DOES NOT DELIGHT IN EVIL BUT REJOICES WITH THE TRUTH. IT ALWAYS PROTECTS, ALWAYS TRUSTS, ALWAYS HOPES, ALWAYS PERSEVERES.

LOVE NEVER FAILS.

23 GIFTS

| Don't neglect.

| Stewards.

| Clarity.

| Meaning and connection.

| Church health.

DEBRIEFING GIFTS

Character of Christ...fruit of the spirit...spiritual disciplines vs. gifting.

Knowing your gifts can focus your "yes" or "no."

Assessment vs. aspects of gifts vs. confusion between roles and gifts.

Gifts are not natural talents:

| Common grace.

| Offer all of yourself.

YOUR TOP 3-5 GIFTS

| Get feedback.

| Awareness.

GOD'S WORD SAYS, ABOUT GIFTS:

• TOLD NOT TO NEGLECT THEM (1 TIMOTHY 4:14); TO NOT BE UNINFORMED
(1 CORINTHIANS 12:1).
• WE ARE STEWARDS OF WHAT GOD'S GIVEN US…AND WILL BE HELD ACCOUNTABLE
(1 PETER 4:10; MATTHEW 25:14-30).

AND

• ONCE YOU KNOW AND USE YOUR SPIRITUAL GIFTS…YOU MAY GET CLEARER ON YOUR
CALLING.
• YOUR MINISTRY CAN FEEL MORE MEANINGFUL AS YOU USE YOUR GIFTS AND FEEL
CONNECTED TO WHAT GOD IS DOING THROUGH AND AROUND YOU.
• "THERE IS MORE UNITY AND OVERALL HEALTH IN CHURCHES THAT TEACH AND
DEVELOP GIFT-BASED MINISTRIES." (BRUCE BUGBEE, NETWORK MINISTRIES
INTERNATIONAL)

DEBRIEFING GIFTS—FAQS

SCRIPTURES ARE CLEAR IN TOTAL THAT WE HAVE INDIVIDUAL COLLECTIONS OF GIFTS
AND NO ONE HAS ALL.

AT THE SAME TIME WE ARE ALL SUPPOSED TO EXHIBIT FAITH, GIVING, MERCY, ETC.

AS WE DEVELOP THE CHARACTER OF CHRIST WE ARE TO EXHIBIT MANY BEHAVIORS AND
ALL THE FRUIT OF THE SPIRIT (GALATIANS 5:22-23)

BUT MY EXPERIENCE WITH GIFTS IS THAT IF IT'S A GIFT, IT'S ABOVE AND BEYOND OUR
DILIGENCE AT BEING DISCIPLINED AT SOMETHING.

FOR EXAMPLE: I CAN BE DISCIPLINED ABOUT INTERCESSION BUT FOR PEOPLE WITH THE
GIFT OF INTERCESSION IT IS SO MUCH A PART OF THEIR BEING THAT FOR THEM IT'S LESS
OF A DISCIPLINE AND CLEARLY AN AREA OF GIFTING. (Presenter insert your own example if
this one doesn't ring true for you.)

DEBRIEFING GIFTS

Character of Christ...fruit of the spirit...spiritual disciplines vs. gifting.

Knowing your gifts can focus your "yes" or "no."

Assessment vs. aspects of gifts vs. confusion between roles and gifts.

Gifts are not natural talents:

| Common grace.

| Offer all of yourself.

YOUR TOP 3-5 GIFTS

| Get feedback.

| Awareness.

KNOWING YOUR GIFTS CAN HELP FOCUS WHERE YOU SAY "YES" AND SAY "NO."

WHAT WERE YOUR AREAS OF NON-GIFTING? THERE ARE THOSE WHO ARE SITTING AND WATCHING AND THINKING THERE IS NO ROOM FOR THEM TO SERVE. YOUR "NO" OPENS UP AN OPPORTUNITY FOR SOMEONE ELSE TO SERVE AND USE THEIR GIFTS AND LIVE INTO THEIR CALL. [Presenter share a personal example here if it fits.]

WHAT IF I EXPECTED TO FIND A CERTAIN GIFT IN MY RESULTS, BUT IT DOESN'T SHOW UP? COULD BE FOR ONE OF ANY NUMBER OF REASONS:

- NO SPIRITUAL GIFTS INSTRUMENT IS PERFECT.
- COULD DEPEND ON WHERE YOUR HEAD/HEART WAS WHEN YOU TOOK IT.
- SOME GIFTS HAVE MULTIPLE ASPECTS, AND MAYBE YOUR GIFT IS JUST ONE OF THOSE ASPECTS, LIKE DISCERNMENT CAN BE ABOUT DISCERNING TRUE FROM FALSE TEACHING, OR IT CAN ALSO BE ABOUT DISCERNING SPIRITUAL EVIL.
- OR IT COULD BE THAT IT'S JUST A DISAPPOINTMENT FOR YOU BECAUSE YOU WANTED THAT GIFT AND YOU DON'T TEST FOR IT AND YOU DON'T HAVE IT.
- OR IT COULD BE CONFUSION BETWEEN TITLES OR ROLES AND GIFTS—YOU MAY BE A TEACHER BUT DON'T HAVE THE GIFT OF TEACHING; THINK IN TERMS OF YOUR CONTEXT.

IS IT REALLY TEACHING YOU NEED IN THAT CONTEXT OR SHEPHERDING? MERCY? WISDOM? KNOWLEDGE?

YOU MAY BE A LEADER BUT DON'T HAVE THE GIFT OF LEADERSHIP; WHAT IS YOUR CONTEXT? IS IT REALLY LEADERSHIP YOU NEED FOR THAT CONTEXT OR ADMINISTRATION? FAITH? APOSTLESHIP?

THINK MORE ABOUT WHAT YOU DO...THE ROLE YOU PLAY.

Gifts...

- Not natural talents
- 3-4-5
- Seasons
- Awareness

YOUR UNIQUE DESIGN

DEBRIEFING GIFTS

Character of Christ...fruit of the spirit... spiritual disciplines vs. gifting.

Knowing your gifts can focus your "yes" or "no."

Assessment vs. aspects of gifts vs. confusion between roles and gifts.

Gifts are not natural talents:

Common grace.

Offer all of yourself.

YOUR TOP 3-5 GIFTS

Get feedback.

Awareness.

GIFTS ARE <u>NOT</u> NATURAL TALENTS—WHICH ARE GIVEN AT PHYSICAL BIRTH.

- SPIRITUAL GIFTS ARE GIVEN AT SPIRITUAL BIRTH.
- TALENTS ARE EVIDENCE OF GOD'S COMMON GRACE TO EVERY HUMAN BEING THAT HE HAS CREATED. WE KNOW PEOPLE WHO DON'T KNOW JESUS BUT WHO ARE BORN WITH INCREDIBLE MUSICAL ABILITY OR TALENT FOR COMMUNICATION ETC.

SO, YOU MAY HAVE A TALENT THAT'S DEVELOPED OR MAYBE INNATE BUT IT ISN'T NECESSARILY USED IN THE CONTEXT OF GOD USING YOU IN A SPECIAL WAY TO GLORIFY HIM AND BUILD UP THE BODY.

- WHAT'S SOMETIMES HARD TO TELL IS THAT WHEN WE BECOME A BELIEVER GOD MAY CHOOSE TO USE EXACTLY THAT ABILITY AND TRANSFORM IT INTO A GIFT--SO A TALENT IN MUSIC BECOMES THE ARTISTIC EXPRESSION GIFT BUT NOT ALWAYS.
- SINCE GOD HAS CALLED THE WHOLE OF YOU TO THE WHOLE OF HIM, DON'T GET TOO WRAPPED UP IN WHETHER IT'S A TALENT OR A GIFT. IF YOU'RE A BELIEVER, YOU'RE CALLED TO OFFER EVERYTHING BACK TO HIM. MAYBE YOU DON'T TEST FOR THE GIFT OF ADMINISTRATION BUT YOU'RE PRETTY ORGANIZED, SO BRING THAT TO THE TABLE.

AND, TYPICALLY, EACH PERSON HAS A CONSTELLATION OF 3-4-5 GIFTS. IF YOU HAVE MANY HIGH SCORES OR A NUMBER THAT ARE TIED, CONSIDER ASKING OTHERS WHO KNOW YOU WELL TO GIVE YOU FEEDBACK ON WHAT THEY THINK YOUR GIFTS ARE. THIS MAY HELP TO SORT OUT YOUR TOP GIFTS.

THERE ALSO SEEM TO BE SCENARIOS WHERE MAYBE GOD HAS GIVEN YOU A GIFT FOR A SEASON... WHAT WE CAN'T TELL FROM SCRIPTURE IS ARE ALL OF YOUR GIFTS GIVEN TO YOU AT THE TIME OF CONVERSION OR DO THEY SHOW UP LATER?--WE DON'T KNOW.

IS THIS A NEW GIFT OR A NEW AWARENESS? I DON'T KNOW THAT WE'RE SUPPOSED TO TOTALLY KNOW. IT'S A PROCESS WHERE FOR THE WHOLE OF YOUR LIFE YOU'RE LIVING INTO WHO GOD HAS MADE YOU TO BE. THIS IS GOD'S PLAN TO USE YOU...ALL OF YOU

[Pause here for questions.]

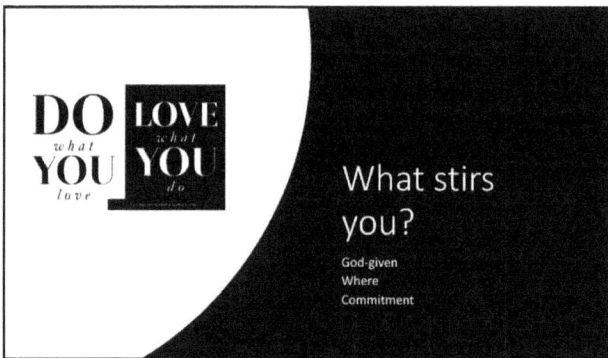

Discovery Exercise

DO what YOU love | LOVE what YOU do

What stirs you?

God-given
Where
Commitment

CLASS GUIDE

Group Exercise

DEBRIEFING GIFTS

EXERCISE:

| TAKE **TWO MINUTES** TO SELECT OR CREATE AN ITEM THAT SYMBOLIZES WHAT YOU REALLY LOVE DOING, OR SOMETHING YOU BELIEVE YOU DO WELL.

| AFTER TWO MINUTES, **SHARE YOUR DISCOVERY** WITH THE OTHERS AT YOUR TABLE.

WHAT STIRS YOU? WHAT MOTIVATES YOU TO MAKE A COMMITTMENT?

TAKE A MOMENT TO JOT DOWN YOUR RESPONSE TO THIS QUESTION: WHAT HINTS ABOUT YOUR INTERESTS OR CALL DID THIS BRIEF EXERCISE UNEARTH OR REAFFIRM FOR YOU?

BUT GIFTS AREN'T THE WHOLE STORY OF GOD'S CALL...

[Need supplies for each table on each table--magazines with lots of photos, construction paper, markers, crayons, yarn, tape, glue-stick, Playdoh, Legos, clay, chenille sticks/pipe-cleaners, etc.]

LET'S TRY A SIMPLE, QUICK DISCOVERY EXERCISE:

IN THE BAG ON YOUR TABLES, YOU'LL FIND A VARIETY OF SUPPLIES.

- **TAKE TWO MINUTES** TO SELECT OR CREATE AN ITEM THAT SYMBOLIZES WHAT YOU REALLY LOVE DOING, OR SOMETHING YOU BELIEVE YOU DO WELL.
- **AFTER TWO MINUTES,** I'LL CALL TIME AND YOU'LL SHARE YOUR DISCOVERY WITH THE OTHERS AT YOUR TABLE.

[Allow 4-6 minutes for sharing]

THIS SIMPLE EXERCISE LIKELY TOLD YOU SOMETHING ABOUT WHAT YOU ENJOY OR WHAT MOTIVATES YOU... AND THE VERY DIFFERENT (OR SIMILAR) INTERESTS OF THE OTHERS AT YOUR TABLE.

WHAT STIRS YOU?

IN ADDITION TO GIFTS (AND TALENTS), GOD HAS ALSO MADE US CARE DEEPLY ABOUT A FEW THINGS. **WE ARE INDIVIDUALLY MOTIVATED BY CERTAIN PEOPLE OR ISSUES OR CAUSES**—MORE SO THAN MATTERS THAT SEEM TO INSPIRE OTHERS. WHAT STIRS OR DRIVES OR INTERESTS YOU CAN BE A GOOD INDICATOR OF WHERE GOD MAY BE CALLING YOU TO GET INVOLVED.

- WE DON'T ALL CARE ABOUT EVERYTHING EQUALLY.
- THINK ABOUT THOSE PLACES YOU FEEL COMPELLED TO MAKE A COMMITMENT.

SOMETIMES IDENTIFYING SIMPLE THINGS LIKE ENJOYING COOKING OR BEING A RUNNING ENTHUSIAST OR WORKING WITH CHILDREN OR LIKING TRAVEL...OR WHATEVER KIND OF THING YOU JUST SHARED WITH YOUR TABLE...**SHOWS PART OF OUR HEARTS, OUR TENDENCIES.** THEY MAY HELP US WHEN WE ARE CONFUSED ABOUT GOD'S CALL. **THINK ABOUT IT AS A SMALL STEP TOWARD WHAT MIGHT BE GOD'S DIRECTION.**

FOR EXAMPLE: **ENJOYING COOKING** MIGHT MEAN THAT IT FEEDS YOUR SOUL AND

Individually answer

What hints about your interests or call did this brief exercise unearth or reaffirm for you?

FOOT LEG · INNER EAR · HEART · MOUTH · HAND ARM · EYE · HEAD · STOMACH KIDNEY LUNG GUT

Putting it All Together

CLASS GUIDE

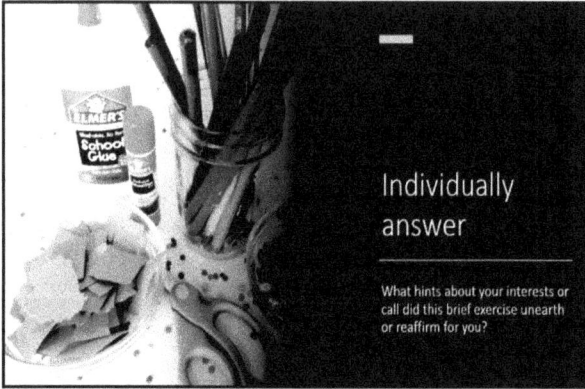

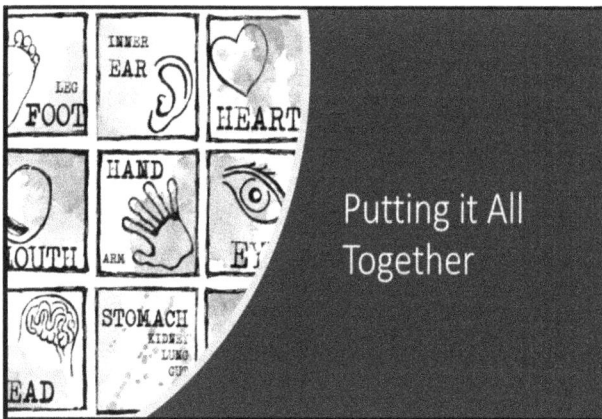

Gifts, Interests, Talents, Experience:
A Lifetime of Serving

IT ALL COUNTS

Gifts are the equipment God gives you to use to accomplish His purposes.

Call and motivation help you determine where and with whom you will serve.

Your unique behavioral style helps shape what your service looks like.

Talent(s) and life experience(s) add richness and direction.

APPLICATION

Affirmation.

New understanding/clarity and seeking a new place to serve.

Permission to focus efforts.

Confusion or need for more learning/discipleship.

BODY IN SUCH A WAY THAT YOU ARE ENERGIZED TO THEN SERVE; OR IT MIGHT MEAN THAT YOU CAN USE THAT PASSION TO BAKE MUFFINS AND TAKE THEM TO SOMEONE IN A NURSING HOME WHO WOULD ENJOY THEM; OR YOU MIGHT TAKE A MEAL TO A NEW MOM; OR MAYBE SERVE IN A SOUP KITCHEN; MAYBE YOU COULD USE THAT PASSION TO TEACH TEENS HOW TO COOK; OR OFFER A NUTRITION AND COOKING CLASS AT THE LOCAL HOME FOR PREGNANT GIRLS.

TAKE A MOMENT TO JOT DOWN YOUR RESPONSE TO THIS QUESTION:
WHAT HINTS ABOUT YOUR INTERESTS OR CALL DID THIS BRIEF TABLE EXERCISE UNEARTH OR REAFFIRM FOR YOU?

GIFTS, PASSION, STYLE—A LIFETIME OF SERVING
INCLUDING OTHER FACTORS: AVAILABILITY, MATURITY, INTERESTS, TALENTS, ETC.

THE IDEA IS THAT THE MORE YOU KNOW OF YOURSELF AND HOW GOD HAS DESIGNED AND CALLED AND GIFTED YOU, THE MORE YOU WILL KNOW YOUR SPIRITUAL JOB DESCRIPTION.

USE GIFTS AS A FILTER FOR YOUR "YES" AND "NO." YOUR GIFTS ARE WHAT YOU DO WHEN YOU ARE SERVING. YOU ADMINISTRATE OR GIVE OR ARE HOSPITABLE OR EXTEND MERCY, ETC.

YOUR CALL AND WHAT MOTIVATES YOU PROVIDE CLUES TO HELP YOU DETERMINE WHERE AND WITH WHOM YOU WILL SERVE.

AND, TAKE TIME TO UNDERSTAND YOUR OWN UNIQUE BEHAVIORAL STYLE—HOW YOU RELATE TO THE WORLD AROUND YOU. ARE YOU MORE TASK OR MORE PEOPLE-ORIENTED? ARE YOU BOLD OR GENTLE IN YOUR APPROACH TO LIFE? **THESE THINGS WILL ALSO SHAPE HOW YOU GET INVOLVED AND WHAT THAT INVOLVEMENT LOOKS LIKE.**

AND REMEMBER, GOD USES EVERYTHING—SO DON'T IGNORE A TALENT YOU HAVE OR A LIFE EXPERIENCE THAT MAKES YOU UNIQUELY SUITED FOR SOMETHING. IT ALL COUNTS.

Putting it Together

- Affirmation?
- Clarity?
- Boundaries?
- Need for Jesus?

Gifts, Interests, Talents, Experience: A Lifetime of Serving

IT ALL COUNTS

Gifts are the equipment God gives you to use to accomplish His purposes.

Call and motivation help you determine where and with whom you will serve.

Your unique behavioral style helps shape what your service looks like.

Talent(s) and life experience(s) add richness and direction.

APPLICATION

Affirmation.

New understanding/clarity and seeking a new place to serve.

Permission to focus efforts.

Confusion or need for more learning/discipleship.

MOSES' CALL WAS TO LEAD GOD'S PEOPLE OUT OF SLAVERY IN EGYPT TO THE PROMISED LAND. MOSES SEEMED TO HAVE A PASSION FOR RESCUING THE HELPLESS (KILLING THE EGYPTIAN WHO WAS BEATING A HEBREW; THEN CHASING OFF THE SHEPHERDS WHO WERE HARASSING THE SHEPHERDESSES). MOSES HAD GIFTS OF LEADERSHIP AND PROPHECY AND WISDOM. HIS OBEDIENCE LOOKED LIKE FREEING THE ISRAELITES AS HE RELIED ON GOD TO USE HIM.

OR THE APOSTLE PAUL. HE WAS ALWAYS RELIGIOUSLY ZEALOUS. ONCE HE CAME TO FOLLOW JESUS CHRIST, GOD USED PAUL'S INTENSITY AND ADDED GIFTS OF TEACHING, EVANGELISM, APOSTLESHIP AND TONGUES, AND USED PAUL TO SPREAD THE GOSPEL MESSAGE AND PLANT NEW CHURCHES.

NOW, WE'RE GOING TO SPEND SOME TIME BRAINSTORMING WITH ONE ANOTHER ABOUT WHERE OUR GIFTS MIGHT BE PUT TO USE. ALWAYS WHEN GIFTS ARE ASSESSED AND TALKED ABOUT, PEOPLE HAVE FEARS AROUND BEING PRESSURED TO GET INVOLVED. I ASSURE YOU THAT IS NOT WHAT THIS IS:

- **FOR SOME, THE GIFTS CONVERSATION IS SIMPLY AN AFFIRMATION** THAT YOU ARE ALREADY IN THE RIGHT PLACE DOING THE THINGS THAT GOD HAS CALLED/GIFTED YOU TO DO. AFFIRMATION IS A GREAT THING!

- **FOR OTHERS, THIS IS A GREAT AHA MOMENT WHERE YOU HAVE GAINED CLARITY** AROUND GOD'S CALL AND REALLY NEED SOME OPTIONS FOR GETTING INVOLVED—SO A LIST OF OPPORTUNITIES OR BRAINSTORMING WITH OTHERS IS USEFUL.

- FOR ADDITIONAL ONES OF YOU, THE STUDY OF GIFTS HAS HELPED YOU COME TO REALIZE THAT **YOU ARE OVERLY BUSY AND TOO INVOLVED** IN TOO MANY THINGS OUT OF A SENSE OF GUILT RATHER THAN CALL...AND THIS GIVES YOU PERMISSION TO QUIT SOMETHING.

- FOR YET OTHERS, YOU FIND THAT THIS CONVERSATION IS CONFUSING BECAUSE **YOU HAVEN'T YET GIVEN YOUR LIFE TO JESUS** AND THAT'S YOUR NEXT STEP. AND, FOR YOU, FINDING EASY-ENTRY SERVING OPPORTUNITIES WHERE YOU CAN SERVE AND BE DISCIPLED CAN BE A GREAT NEXT STEP.

Helping Identify Possible Areas for Ministry

In your small groups:
- Help each other discern gifts and call and stirrings
- Spend time helping each other brainstorm ideas for serving...or focusing ministry
- Might be helpful to think about: if you are serving, what do you love about it? Or, if you are seeking to serve, what are you looking for in a serving opportunity?

Resources
- Pray
- Bible
- Ministry opportunities in your church
- Ministry opportunities in your community
- Announcements/posts
- Coaching
- Staff support

YOUR UNIQUE DESIGN

Group Exercise

HELPING EACH OTHER IDENTIFY POSSIBLE AREAS OF MINISTRY

TABLE DISCUSSION GUIDE:

| Help each other discern gifts and call and interests.

| Spend time helping each other brainstorm ideas for serving or focusing ministry. It might be helpful to think about: if you are serving, what do you love about it? Or if you are seeking to serve, what are you looking for in a serving opportunity...and where do your gifts fit?

JOT DOWN IDEAS FOR YOUR OWN SERVICE/ENGAGEMENT BELOW:

WHAT IS ONE STEP YOU CAN TAKE NOW?

CLASS GUIDE

OTHER RESOURCES

| Prayer.
| Bible.
| Your class leader.
| Your church website.
| Local nonprofit agencies and human services organizations.
| Keep an eye on your church bulletin newsletter weekly posts and worship announcements.
| Meet with a Gifts Coach.
| Do the six-week *God. Gifts. You. Your Unique Calling and Design* study with your small group. Available at GODGIFTSYOU.COM

ADDITIONAL GUIDANCE

| Try something!
| Recognize that it's a process.
| Don't give up.
| Your first response.
| Visible to others.
| Don't let guilt be a motivator.

1 PETER 4:10 | Each of you should use whatever gift you have received to serve others, as faithful stewards of God's grace in its various forms.

| Stewards of grace.

| In God's strength.

JOT DOWN what you want to remember from this session, or answer: In what ways are you feeling challenged about the discovery or use of your ministry gift(s)?

SMALL GROUP EXERCISE—HELPING EACH OTHER IDENTIFY MINISTRY POSSIBILITIES

[Presenter give an example of how to put—or how YOU have put--gifts and passion and life experience together.]

TABLE DISCUSSION GUIDE:
-- HELP EACH OTHER DISCERN GIFTS AND CALL AND PASSION.
-- SPEND TIME HELPING EACH OTHER BRAINSTORM IDEAS FOR SERVING.

[IT MIGHT BE HELPFUL TO THINK ABOUT: IF YOU ARE SERVING, WHAT DO YOU LOVE ABOUT IT? OR, IF YOU ARE SEEKING TO SERVE, WHAT ARE YOU LOOKING FOR IN A SERVING OPPORTUNITY?]
[Allow 10-15 min.]

REMEMBER OUR WHOLE LIVES ARE SERVICE—SO MAYBE THIS IS A MOMENT WHERE GOD CAN OPEN YOUR EYES TO HOW YOU ARE USING OR CAN BEST USE YOUR GIFTS IN YOUR CURRENT CONTEXTS.

[Call back together]

RESOURCES

[Presenter: revise this list - and slide - as needed for your context.]
SOME RESOURCES FOR YOU AS YOU CONTINUE TO SEEK WHAT GOD WOULD HAVE YOU DO NEXT:
-- PRAY—ASK GOD TO SHOW YOU EACH DAY HOW HE WANTS TO USE YOU.
-- READ THE BIBLE—THE INSIGHTS GLEANED THERE ARE INVALUABLE ON YOUR JOURNEY, AND CAN HELP CORRECT ANY MISPERCEPTIONS.
-- MINISTRY OPPORTUNITIES IN YOUR CHURCH.
-- MINISTRY OPPORTUNITIES IN THE COMMUNITY.
-- KEEP AN EYE ON THE BULLETIN AND WORSHIP ANNOUNCEMENTS.
-- MEET WITH A GIFTS COACH.
-- CONTACT OUR EQUIPPING MINISTRY STAFF [Add contact information.]

EVERY GIFT IS NOT JUST FOR US TO USE, IT'S A REFLECTION OF THE VERY NATURE OF GOD.

YOUR UNIQUE DESIGN: GUIDE

YOUR UNIQUE DESIGN: GUIDE

- Try something
- It's a process
- Don't give up
- No guilt
- Joy...expectation

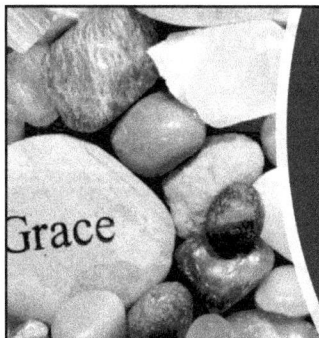

1 Peter 4:10

Each of you should use whatever gift you have received to serve others, as faithful stewards of God's grace in its various forms.

CLASS GUIDE

OTHER RESOURCES

| Prayer.
| Bible.
| Your class leader.
| Your church website.
| Local nonprofit agencies and human services organizations.
| Keep an eye on your church bulletin/newsletter/weekly posts and worship announcements.
| Meet with a Gifts Coach.
| Do the six-week *God. Gifts. You. Your Unique Calling and Design* study with your small group. Available at GODGIFTSYOU.COM

ADDITIONAL GUIDANCE

| Try something!
| Recognize that it's a process.
| Don't give up.
| Your first response.
| Visible to others.
| Don't let guilt be a motivator.

1 PETER 4:10 | Each of you should use whatever gift you have received to serve others, as faithful stewards of God's grace in its various forms.

| Stewards of grace.

| In God's strength.

JOT DOWN what you want to remember from this session, or answer: In what ways are you feeling challenged about the discovery or use of your ministry gift(s)?

64

SOME ADDITIONAL THOUGHTS:

- TRY SOMETHING! STEP OUT IN FAITH AND USE WHAT YOU KNOW ABOUT YOURSELF AND WHAT YOU KNOW ABOUT GOD. TRUST GOD. LEARN AS YOU EXPERIMENT.

REMEMBER: WE CARRY THE PRESENCE AND POWER OF THE HOLY SPIRIT WITHIN US... AND DEVELOPMENT AND USE OF YOUR SPIRITUAL GIFTS MAY DO MORE FOR YOUR GROWTH AS A BELIEVER THAN ANY OTHER SINGLE THING.

- RECOGNIZE THAT IT'S A PROCESS. USING YOUR GIFTS AND UNDERSTANDING THEM WILL TAKE A LIFETIME. GROWING INTO CHRIST-LIKENESS TAKES A LIFETIME.

- TWO INDICATORS THAT WHAT YOU ARE USING IS TRULY A GIFT: IT'S YOUR FIRST RESPONSE IN ANY GIVEN SITUATION (INTERCESSION—YOU PRAY FIRST; MERCY—YOU ARE MERCIFUL WITHOUT EVEN THINKING...) AND OTHERS CAN SEE IT IN ACTION. "YOU ARE SUCH AN ENCOURAGER." "THANK YOU FOR YOUR GIFT OF TEACHING."

- DON'T GIVE UP RIGHT AWAY IF THINGS DON'T WORK OUT EXACTLY AS YOU HAD HOPED THE FIRST OR EVEN THE SECOND TIME. THE EXPERIENCES THAT TEACH YOU WHAT YOUR GIFTS ARE NOT ARE AS VALUABLE ALONG THE WAY AS THE AFFIRMING ONES.

- DON'T LET GUILT BE A MOTIVATOR. IT'S NOT ABOUT BEING BUSIER...IT'S ABOUT DOING WHAT GOD DESIGNED YOU TO DO.

BE MOTIVATED BY JOY...BY EXPECTATION...BY CURIOSITY OF WHAT GOD CAN DO...BY INVITATION. I'D RATHER YOU FEEL CALLED AND SENT THAN PUSHED.

1 PETER 4:10 SAYS "EACH OF YOU SHOULD USE WHATEVER GIFT YOU HAVE RECEIVED TO SERVE OTHERS, AS FAITHFUL STEWARDS OF GOD'S GRACE IN ITS VARIOUS FORMS." OR "LIKE GOOD STEWARDS OF THE MANIFOLD [VARIOUS, DIVERSE, MANY, MULTIPLE, ASSORTED] GRACE OF GOD, SERVE ONE ANOTHER WITH WHATEVER GIFT EACH OF YOU HAS RECEIVED."

1 Peter 4:11

If anyone speaks, they should do so as one who speaks the very words of God. If anyone serves, they should do so with the strength God provides, **so that** in all things God may be praised through Jesus Christ.

CLASS GUIDE

OTHER RESOURCES

Prayer.
Bible.
Your class leader.
Your church website.
Local nonprofit agencies and human services organizations.
Keep an eye on your church bulletin/newsletter/weekly posts and worship announcements.
Meet with a Gifts Coach.
Do the six-week *God Gifts You: Your Unique Calling and Design* study with your small group. Available at GODGIFTSYOU.COM

ADDITIONAL GUIDANCE

Try something!
Recognize that it's a process.
Don't give up.
Your first response.
Visible to others.
Don't let guilt be a motivator.

1 PETER 4:10 Each of you should use whatever gift you have received to serve others, as faithful stewards of God's grace in its various forms.

Stewards of grace.

In God's strength.

JOT DOWN what you want to remember from this session, or answer: In what ways are you feeling challenged about the discovery or use of your ministry gift(s)?

Reflect on

In what ways are you feeling challenged about the discovery or use of your ministry gift(s)?

USING YOUR GIFTS IS NO MORE COMPLICATED THAN BEING STEWARDS OF GOD'S GRACE IN ITS VARIOUS FORMS TO ONE ANOTHER... TO THE GLORY OF JESUS.

DON'T MAKE THIS PROCESS SO COMPLICATED THAT IT PARALYZES YOU OR MAKES YOU THINK THAT YOU ARE WAITING FOR TOTAL CLARITY. JUST DO SOMETHING. GOD WILL TEACH YOU THROUGH THAT. THE FIT AND THE NON-FIT.

1 PETER 4:11 ADDS "IF ANYONE SPEAKS, THEY SHOULD DO SO AS ONE WHO SPEAKS THE VERY WORDS OF GOD. IF ANYONE SERVES, THEY SHOULD DO SO WITH THE STRENGTH GOD PROVIDES, SO THAT IN ALL THINGS GOD MAY BE PRAISED THROUGH JESUS CHRIST. [SO THAT GOD MAY BE GLORIFIED IN ALL THINGS THROUGH JESUS CHRIST]..."

IN GOD'S STRENGTH...AND...GOD RECEIVES THE GLORY

FROM THIS DAY FORTH, I HOPE YOU WILL COMMIT TO FINDING OUT HOW GOD HAS CREATED YOUR INMOST BEING...AND HOW HE HAS SHAPED AND GIFTED YOU TO LIVE AND SERVE...

TAKE A MOMENT ON YOUR OWN...AND JOT DOWN IN YOUR WORKBOOK ON P. 31 ONE OR TWO THINGS YOU WANT TO REMEMBER FROM THIS SESSION.

YOU MIGHT CONSIDER RESPONDING TO THIS QUESTION:

IN WHAT WAYS ARE YOU FEELING CHALLENGED ABOUT THE DISCOVERY OR USE OF YOUR MINISTRY GIFT(S)? (Give 5 min.)

Forms

Class Form—p. 39

Course Evaluation Form —p. 41-42

Involvement Card

APPENDIX B

Your Unique Design: Class Form

Please complete this form and return it to your class leader.

NAME _____ EMAIL / PHONE: _____

Your Spiritual Gifts	Interests/Experience	Ministry Passions
☐ Administration	☐ Art | Media | Theatre | *Specify skills*	☐ Administration | Organizing
☐ Apostleship		☐ Children (Early/ Elementary)
☐ Artistic Expression	☐ Mechanical | *Specify skills*	☐ Emergent | Young/ Adult
☐ Craftsmanship		☐ Facilities
☐ Discernment	☐ Event Planning | *Specify skills*	☐ Youth (Middle/ High School
☐ Evangelism		☐ Connecting | Equipping
☐ Exhortation	☐ Baking | Cooking | Food Service | *Specify skills*	☐ Leadership
☐ Faith		☐ Men's Ministry
☐ Giving	☐ Helping where needed | *Specify skills*	☐ Missions | Outreach
☐ Healing		☐ Music | Worship
☐ Helps	☐ Construction | Contracting | *Specify skills*	☐ Care | Helping | Counseling
☐ Hospitality		☐ Senior Adults
☐ Intercession	☐ General | *Specify skills*	☐ Spiritual Formation | Adult Education
☐ Interpr Tongues	☐ Music | Worship | *Specify skills*	☐ University
☐ Knowledge		☐ Welcoming | Community Life
☐ Leadership	☐ Technical | Office Skills | *Specify skills*	☐ Women's Ministry
☐ Mercy		☐ Other Passion(s)
☐ Miraculous Powers	☐ Professional Services | *Specify skills*	
☐ Prophecy		
☐ Shepherding	☐ Teaching | Facilitating | *Specify groups / ages*	NOTES
☐ Teaching		
☐ Tongues	☐ Other | *Specify skills*	
☐ Wisdom		

Your Unique Design: Course Evaluation

DATE(S) OF THE CLASS(ES) YOU ATTENDED: _____

PLEASE RATE THE MATERIAL PRESENTED IN THE COURSE, USING THE FOLLOWING SCALE

1	2	3	4	5
POOR				EXCELLENT
NOT LIKELY				VERY LIKELY
NOT RELEVANT				VERY RELEVANT

1. How would you rate the value and quality of this course?

2. How was your learning experience in this course?

3. How relevant is what you learned to life/work/ministry?

4. How likely would you be to recommend this course?

5. What aspects of the course were most beneficial?

6. When we present this course again, what should we consider doing differently?

7. If we were to quote you about this class, what would you say?

8. Please comment on the written material provided.

Evaluation continued on the back

YOUR UNIQUE DESIGN _____

PLEASE RATE THE INSTRUCTOR(S), USING THE FOLLOWING SCALE

1	2	3	4	5
POOR				EXCELLENT

INSTRUCTOR 1 NAME: _____

INSTRUCTOR 2 NAME (if applicable): _____

9. To what extent did the instructor(s) demonstrate comfort with and understanding of the material?

INSTRUCTOR 1:

INSTRUCTOR 2:

10. To what extent did the instructor(s)' style and presentation contribute to your learning?

INSTRUCTOR 1:

INSTRUCTOR 2:

11. To what extent did the instructor(s)' interaction with class participants facilitate your learning?

INSTRUCTOR 1:

INSTRUCTOR 2:

12. Additional comments:

Please return this completed form to your class leader.

PLEASE COMPLETE THE FOLLOWING FORMS AND TURN THEM IN TODAY:

    1. YOUR UNIQUE DESIGN CLASS FORM WHICH IS APPENDIX B, P. 39 IN YOUR BOOKS.

    2. YOUR UNIQUE DESIGN COURSE EVALUATION WHICH IS PGS. 41 AND 42.

MAKE REFERENCE TO RESOURCES FOR FOLLOW-UP, RESOURCE TABLE, HOW TO TAKE A NEXT STEP AT YOUR CHURCH...

[Note: you and your team will want to have had a conversation about this prior to offering the Your Unique Design Classes so that you are prepared to connect people to opportunities.]

PRAY

Appendix A

COLORING BOOK PAGE
[COPY FOR SESSION I - 1 COPY PER PERSON]

(SEE REVERSE SIDE OF THIS PAGE - P. 72)

Appendix B

YOUR SPIRITUAL GIFT ASSESSMENT

Please read each statement carefully and give each one a score (from 0 to 5) relative to how well the statement reflects your behavior/experience. Answer how you ARE, not how you want to be. Transfer the numbers to the boxes on the Spiritual Gift Scoring Sheet.

0	1	2	3	4	5
Never true of me					True of me

1. _____ I am good at taking care of details that other people might neglect.
2. _____ I have been successful in starting new ministries.
3. _____ God uses my artistic/musical gifts to help people worship him.
4. _____ I enjoy working with my hands to create things that facilitate my own or another's ministry.
5. _____ When I hear somebody claim to be teaching from the Bible, I can usually tell whether the teaching is sound or unsound.
6. _____ When I talk to non-Christians about Jesus, they are often interested in what I have to say.
7. _____ I am able to motivate others to persevere in the face of discouragement and struggles.
8. _____ I am more confident than most that God will keep his promises.
9. _____ I rearrange things in my life in order to be able to give my financial or other resources more generously to God's work.
10. _____ When there is a job to be done, I am one of the first to jump in and volunteer.
11. _____ In gatherings of people, I tend to notice those at the margins and make them feel like they belong.
12. _____ People who know me consider me a "prayer warrior".
13. _____ Others look to me for my knowledge of Biblical concepts and/or my insight into situations.
14. _____ When the path forward for a group is uncertain, people look to me for leadership.
15. _____ Comforting those who are suffering comes naturally to me.
16. _____ I often say things that people in the church need to hear, even though it may make them uncomfortable.
17. _____ I have been able to successfully guide others in their spiritual journeys.
18. _____ I can usually explain Biblical truth to people in a way that allows them to "get it".
19. _____ People look to me for counsel when there are decisions to be made.
20. _____ When I see people who are sick, I have a strong desire to pray for their healing.
21. _____ I have seen God do something miraculous in connection with a prayer I have prayed.
22. _____ When I pray, sometimes words come out that I don't understand.
23. _____ When someone speaks in Tongues, I am able to understand the message.
24. _____ Others look to me for my organizational skills.

APPENDIX B CONTINUED:

25. _____ When I see a need in the church or community, I envision how to create a ministry to meet the need.
26. _____ I can communicate important things about God to others through writing, art, or music.
27. _____ I am skilled at creating useful items from tangible materials like glass, metal, ceramic, wood, paper, etc.
28. _____ I can tell when there is spiritual evil in a situation.
29. _____ Sharing the Gospel comes easily to me.
30. _____ People think of me as an encouraging friend.
31. _____ In the face of doubt or uncertainty, I persevere in doing the things God has called me to do.
32. _____ I frequently look for opportunities to contribute money or resources in a way that makes a difference.
33. _____ I don't particularly care what I'm doing to serve, as long as it helps further God's work in the church or the world.
34. _____ Either in my home or elsewhere, I create a welcoming atmosphere for others.
35. _____ When I learn about somebody in a difficult situation, my first impulse is to pray.
36. _____ I see the shades of gray in situations where others see black and white.
37. _____ I motivate others to come along with me as I pursue God's vision.
38. _____ My automatic response when someone is hurting is to come alongside and offer a listening ear and a shoulder to cry on.
39. _____ God sometimes leads me to ask difficult questions and point out inconvenient truths.
40. _____ I enjoy coming alongside someone in one-on-one mentoring.
41. _____ I am able to connect the God's truth with today's life situations.
42. _____ I can usually see the wise course of action to take.
43. _____ I have seen God heal someone in connection with a prayer I have prayed or by my laying on of hands.
44. _____ I have sometimes felt powerfully led by God to perform an extraordinary act.
45. _____ Praying privately in tongues builds my personal faith and helps me feel closer to God.
46. _____ I am able to provide the meaning of a message of Tongues to others present.
47. _____ If somebody has a good vision, I can do the work of putting it into practice.
48. _____ I have been told I exhibit an entrepreneurial capacity.
49. _____ I express something of God's creativity through dance, written communication, painting, drawing, or drama.
50. _____ Others depend on me to make or fix things.
51. _____ Others have told me that I have a strong intuitive sense, seeing dangers or opportunities that others miss.
52. _____ I actively develop relationships with and reach out to those outside the church community.
53. _____ I enjoy helping people take steps toward greater maturity in any aspect of their lives.

APPENDIX B CONTINUED:

54. _____ In situations where others might doubt God, I do not.

55. _____ Although my generosity is usually meant to be anonymous, people know me as charitable and philanthropic with the resources God has given me.

56. _____ I enjoy doing the behind-the-scenes things that support others' ministries.

57. _____ Others have noticed that I am good at making people feel welcome and accepted wherever I go.

58. _____ I am one of the first people others turn to when asking for prayer.

59. _____ I often see important aspects of Biblical passages that others do not recognize.

60. _____ I inspire others to pursue goals that I clearly articulate.

61. _____ People describe me as compassionate and empathic.

62. _____ God uses me to point out his plans and purposes when others may be straying from the path.

63. _____ I find satisfaction in long-term coaching relationships.

64. _____ Others have consistently said that they have learned from or been challenged by my teaching.

65. _____ I am rarely confused about what next steps to take in challenging situations.

66. _____ I am drawn to participate in ministries like "inner healing prayer" or "spiritual deliverance healing."

67. _____ God has authenticated a message or ministry by working through me to perform something supernatural.

68. _____ I have spoken about faith in a language that is not my native tongue, and felt like God was enabling my fluency.

69. _____ If someone prays in Tongues, I get a feeling or vision or picture of what the message means.

APPENDIX B CONTINUED:

YOUR SPIRITUAL GIFT ASSESSMENT SCORING SHEET

- Please record your scores from the previous two pages onto this chart.
  - **Pay attention to the question numbering.**
- Total each column to get a number for each letter.
- Circle your top 3-5 scores (looking at A through W).
- Note your lowest 2 scores (just looking at A through S).
- Turn to the next page to find your corresponding gifts (and non-gifts).

1.	2.	3.	4.	5.	6.	7.	8.	9.	10.	11.	12.
24.	25.	26.	27.	28.	29.	30.	31.	32.	33.	34.	35.
47.	48.	49.	50.	51.	52.	53.	54.	55.	56.	57.	58.
A.	B.	C.	D.	E.	F.	G.	H.	I.	J.	K.	L.

13.	14.	15.	16.	17.	18.	19.	20.	21.	22.	23.
36.	37.	38.	39.	40.	41.	42.	43.	44.	45.	46.
59.	60.	61.	62.	63.	64.	65.	66.	67.	68.	69.
M.	N.	O.	P.	Q.	R.	S.	T.	U.	V.	W.

APPENDIX B CONTINUED:

Spiritual Gifts	Record Your Top 3-5 Scores (A – W):	List Your Lower 2 Scores (A - S):	Which gifts do others affirm you have?
A = Administration			
B = Apostleship			
C = Artistic Expression			
D = Craftsmanship			
E = Discernment			
F = Evangelism			
G = Exhortation			
H = Faith			
I = Giving			
J = Helps			
K = Hospitality			
L = Intercession			
M = Knowledge			
N = Leadership			
O = Mercy			
P = Prophecy			
Q = Shepherding			
R = Teaching			
S = Wisdom			
T = Healing			
U = Miraculous Powers			
V = Tongues			
W = Interpretation of Tongues			

Appendix C

SPIRITUAL GIFTS OVERVIEW

Gift	Brief Definition: Those with gifts of _____...:	Descriptors:	Name Someone You Think Has This Gift:
Administration	...bring efficiency and order to the church and to other organizations. These are usually the planners, goal-setters, or managers. They look for new ways to help people and tasks be more effective.	Organizer Strategizer Developer	
Apostleship	...introduce new ministries to the church. They blaze new trails, pioneer new endeavors, and step out into uncharted territory. They may have a great desire to reach out to unreached peoples and to spread the vision of the mission of the church.	Starter Entrepreneur Pioneer	
Artistic Expression	...have a special ability to communicate God's message through the fine arts, including drama, creative writing, music, and drawing. Through their God-given creativity, theyuse their gifts to draw others in and focus on God, His creation, and His message to us.	Expressive Innovative Creative	
Craftsmanship	...are uniquely skilled at working with raw materials, helping to create things that are used for ministry or that help meet tangible needs. They can be found fixing, remodeling, and sprucing up buildings, and/or creating and stitching items—honoring God and benefitting His people in practical ways.	Creative Skilled Resourceful	
Discernment	...distinguish between good and evil, truth and error, right and wrong. These people provide much-needed insight, point out inconsistencies in teaching God's Word, challenge deceitfulness in others, help sort out impure motives from pure ones, and identify spiritual warfare.	Intuitive Perceptive Sensitive	

APPENDIX C CONTINUED:

Gift	Brief Definition: Those with gifts of _____...:	Descriptors:	Name Someone You Think Has This Gift:
Evangelism	...seem to be always seeking to build meaningful relationships with non-believers and are often able to steer conversations with these people to spiritual things. They communicate the good news of Jesus to unbelievers in such a way that they see people believe and commit to following Christ.	Forthright Influential Heart for the lost	
Exhortation	...offer a word of hope combined with a gentle push to action to those who are discouraged, tentative, or needing direction. People with this gift come alongside to offer reassurance and affirmation, and, when needed, to challenge or confront, all with the goal of seeing others grow to greater maturity in their faith.	Affirming Motivator Heartening	
Faith	...have that extra measure of confidence in God and His promises, helping inspire others to greater belief. Those with this gift live constantly in the knowledge that God works all things for their good and the good of others who are called according to His purposes.	Believing Hopeful Secure	
Giving	...have an extra measure of the ability to be generous. People with this gift live as if everything they have belongs to God, knowing that God will provide for their needs. Giving may involve money as well as other resources like housing, food, clothing, etc.	Resourceful Sacrificial Steward	
Helps	...meet the practical needs of others and of the church/organizations in order to enhance, support, or accomplish ministry. Indicators of someone with the gift of helps are that he/she serves willingly, cheerfully, humbly, and wherever needed.	Humble Available Dependable	
Hospitality	...have the divine ability to make people feel welcome and accepted--anywhere at any time. People with this gift enjoy connecting people with each other and creating an atmosphere where relationships and community can flourish.	Accepting Welcoming Friendly	

Gift	Brief Definition: Those with gifts of _____...:	Descriptors:	Name Someone You Think Has This Gift:
Intercession	...feel compelled by God to pray on a daily basis for others. They are completely convinced of the awesome power and necessity of prayer. They pray as a first response to any given situation, during that situation, and afterwards.	Faithful Trusting Aware	
Knowledge	...bring Biblical truth and God-given insight to the church. They may also receive a word from God that is uniquely timed and tailored for a given situation. People with the gift of knowledge may also be those who have a keen desire to study and know God's Word, and God may use this understanding of Scripture to speak a word of knowledge to a person or group.	Aware Perceptive Student of Scripture	
Leadership	...are visionary, good motivators, and effective directors—helping inspire others to achieve God's purpose. Leadership involves not only having a vision of the preferred future for the church or an organization, but also having clarity on next steps to achieve that vision, the ability to communicate vision in a way that inspires others, and the ability to equip the rest of the team to pursue the same direction together.	Visionary Goal-oriented Credible	
Mercy	...provide comfort, support, and presence to those who are suffering, in crisis, or otherwise hurting. Those with this gift reach out to others who are broken, having themselves experienced God in their own brokenness. They show God's heart to those who need the empathy of a listening ear.	Caring Compassionate Kind	
Prophecy	...have the gift that God uses to convict His people of sin and their need for repentance. Prophecy brings warning, challenge, correction, and confrontation without compromise.	Exposes Challenges Bold	
Shepherding	...provide nurture and guidance to others so that they grow in spiritual maturity and Christ-like character. People with the shepherding gift seek to walk alongside someone for a long or short season and direct them to Jesus and His offer of life, hope, and peace.	Fosters health Guide Counselor	

APPENDIX C CONTINUED:

Gift	Brief Definition: Those with gifts of _____...:	Descriptors:	Name Someone You Think Has This Gift:
Teaching	...study, understand, explain, and apply Scripture's truths in such a way that people grow in their own understanding, are challenged, and are inspired to apply what they've learned. This can be done in a church or other context, since God's truth is true everywhere.	Communicator Inspiring Applies learning	
Wisdom	...use their God-given insight and information by applying it to specific situations, providing guidance in the church. They see the right course of action in the midst of otherwise confusing or overwhelming circumstances. Input from those with wisdom can shift a group's direction or help guide someone toward greater clarity.	Guide Perceptive Good judgment	
Healing	...follow the pattern we see in the life and ministry of Jesus where healing was physical, mental, emotional, and/or spiritual. Often also used by God to authenticate a message or a ministry. Always it is to show God's grace and mercy and power.	Restorer Responsive Intercessor	
Miraculous Powers	...help authenticate a ministry, encourage a body of believers, and show the power of God. In the life and ministry of Jesus, His miracles included feeding the multitudes, turning water into wine, raising the dead and walking on water.	Responsive Courageous Alert	
Tongues	...may speak in other languages as the Spirit enables them (Acts 2); may speak in an unknown language (that of "angels"-1 Cor. 13); may speak to God in tongues (1 Cor. 13). It can also be a way of "uttering the mysteries of the Spirit," and "sounding a clear call" to God's people (1 Cor. 14). Usually accompanied Interpretation of Tongues gift.	Responsive Expressive Worshipful	
Interpretation of Tongues	...help the rest of the Body of Christ understand the message being spoken by those with the gift of Tongues. May be given concurrently to someone with Tongues.	Responsive Obedient Discerning	

Appendix D

FINDING GIFTS IN SCRIPTURE

1. For the following three passages, circle the activities you note and jot down a possible theme that you see in all three.

Praise him with the sounding of the trumpet, praise him with the harp and lyre, praise him with timbrel and dancing, praise him with the strings and pipe, praise him with the clash of cymbals, praise him with resounding cymbals (Psalm 150:3-5).

Then Miriam the prophet, Aaron's sister, took a timbrel in her hand, and all the women followed her, with timbrels and dancing. Miriam sang to them: "Sing to the Lord, for he is highly exalted. Both horse and driver he has hurled into the sea" (Exodus 15:20-21).

Wearing a linen ephod, David was dancing before the Lord with all his might, while he and all Israel were bringing up the ark of the Lord with shouts and the sound of trumpets (2 Samuel 6:14-15).

2. For the following three passages, what is the gift mentioned or implied?

Epaphras, who is one of you and a servant of Christ Jesus, sends greetings. He is always wrestling in prayer for you, that you may stand firm in all the will of God, mature and fully assured (Colossians 4:12).

I have not stopped giving thanks for you, remembering you in my prayers (Ephesians 1:16).

I thank God, whom I serve, as my ancestors did, with a clear conscience, as night and day I constantly remember you in my prayers (2 Timothy 1:3).

APPENDIX D CONTINUED:

3. Circle the spiritual gifts mentioned or implied in each of the following passages.

Now the Lord spoke to Moses, saying, "See, I have called by name Bezalel, the son of Uri, the son of Hur, of the tribe of Judah. I have filled him with the Spirit of God in wisdom, in understanding, in knowledge, and in all kinds of craftsmanship, to make artistic designs for work in gold, in silver, and in bronze, and in the cutting of stones for settings, and in the carving of wood, that he may work in all kinds of craftsmanship (Exodus 31:1-5, NASB).

Now to each one the manifestation of the Spirit is given for the common good. To one there is given through the Spirit a message of wisdom, to another a message of knowledge by means of the same Spirit, to another faith by the same Spirit, to another gifts of healing by that one Spirit, to another miraculous powers, to another prophecy, to another distinguishing between spirits, to another speaking in different kinds of tongues [languages] and to still another the interpretation of tongues [languages]. All these are the work of one and the same Spirit, and he distributes them to each one, just as he determines (1 Corinthians 12:7-11).

Now you are the body of Christ, and each one of you is a part of it. And God has placed in the church first of all apostles, second prophets, third teachers, then miracles, then gifts of healing, of helping, of guidance, and of different kinds of tongues. Are all apostles? Are all prophets? Are all teachers? Do all work miracles? Do all have gifts of healing? Do all speak in tongues [languages]? Do all interpret? (1 Corinthians 12:27-30).

Offer hospitality to one another without grumbling. Each of you should use whatever gift you have received to serve others, as faithful stewards of God's grace in its various forms. If anyone speaks, they should do so as one who speaks the very words of God. If anyone serves, they should do so with the strength God provides, so that in all things God may be praised through Jesus Christ. To him be the glory and the power for ever and ever. Amen (1 Peter 4:9-11).

For just as each of us has one body with many members, and these members do not all have the same function, so in Christ we, though many, form one body, and each member belongs to all the others. We have different gifts, according to the grace given to each of us. If your gift is prophesying, then prophesy in accordance with your faith; if it is serving, then serve; if it is teaching, then teach; if it is to encourage, then give encouragement; if it is giving, then give generously; if it is to lead, do it diligently; if it is to show mercy, do it cheerfully (Romans 12:4-8).

APPENDIX D CONTINUED:

Some of us have been given special ability as apostles; to others he has given the gift of being able to preach well; some have special ability in winning people to Christ, helping them to trust him as their Savior; still others have a gift for caring for God's people as a shepherd does his sheep, leading and teaching them in the ways of God. Why is it that he gives us these special abilities to do certain things best? It is that God's people will be equipped to do better work for him, building up the Church, the body of Christ, to a position of strength and maturity; until finally we all believe alike about our salvation and about our Savior, God's Son, and all become full-grown in the Lord—yes, to the point of being filled full with Christ (Ephesians 4:11-13; NLT).

Appendix E

_____ **(Ministry/Job Title)**

IMPORTANCE TO CHURCH

The Mission of _____(Name of Ministry) is to (insert Mission statement for your ministry area) _____

BENEFIT TO PERSON SERVING

- Use of spiritual gifts in service to God and the Body of Christ at (insert church/faith organization name).
- Be a part of making (organization name) a more (insert descriptors) place.
- Fellowship and ministry with other like-minded believers.
- See God at work in and through you and (insert Ministry name).
- (Add any other benefits).

RESPONSIBILITIES

- (List any and all responsibilities—Participate? Coordinate? Organize? Plan? Etc.

TIME COMMITMENT

- (Be specific here—is this daily/weekly/monthly/quarterly? How many hours total?)
- (Also—is it location-specific or can it be done from home? From anywhere?)

SKILLS/KNOWLEDGE/EXPERIENCE

- (List the primary skills, knowledge, and experience require for the position.)
- (Add skills, knowledge, experience desired, but perhaps not required.)
- Desired spiritual gifts for this position: (list gifts).
- (Does this person need to be a member of your church/organization—list that here).
- (Does this person need to complete training, classes, certifications, background checks, etc.?)

RESOURCES/TRAINING/ACCOUNTABILITY

- Support from (List staff and ministry leaders who will provide support for this person).
- Training and resources for particular ministry area provided. (You may wish to be more specific here).

SELECTION PROCESS

- (Is this position one where anyone can sign up or by invitation only? Be clear. If it is by invitation, list who does the inviting—a Pastor, a Director, another team member?)

POSITIONS AVAILABLE

- (Are you looking for 2 people or 20 people?)

RESPONSIBLE TO

- (List the name and title of the person to whom this volunteer will be responsible.)

_____ (Ministry/Job Title)

IMPORTANCE TO CHURCH

BENEFIT TO PERSON SERVING
-
-
-
-

RESPONSIBILITIES
-
-
-

TIME COMMITMENT
-
-

SKILLS/KNOWLEDGE/EXPERIENCE
-
-
-

RESOURCES/TRAINING/ACCOUNTABILITY
-
-
-

SELECTION PROCESS
-

POSITIONS AVAILABLE
-

RESPONSIBLE TO
-

About the Author

SHIRLEY GILES DAVIS, AUTHOR OF THE *GOD. GIFTS. YOU. YOUR UNIQUE CALLING AND DESIGN* **WORKBOOK,** is a consultant, coach, and facilitator who has worked with faith-based groups, nonprofit agencies, and leaders in a diversity of organizations for over 30 years. Shirley has been the Catalyst for Equipping of a 1200 member church in Boulder, Colorado since 1999.

RESOURCES:
- Your Unique Design Class Guide
- God. Gifts. You.: Your Unique Calling and Design
- DIOS. DONES. TÚ.: Tu llamado y diseño único (Spanish Edition)
- GodGiftsYou.com
- Gifts-Calling-Purpose Blog

YOU CAN FIND THESE EITHER ON AMAZON OR THROUGH GODGIFTSYOU.COM.

www.ingramcontent.com/pod-product-compliance
Lightning Source LLC
LaVergne TN
LVHW061301060426
835509LV00016B/1671